IN
GOD'S
WAITING
ROOM

mikki dehart

Turning Scars into Stars
Confessions of the Soul

Contents

Acknowledgements   Page 1

Introduction   Page 4

Forward   Page 7

1 In God's Waiting Room   Page 10

#2 Vulnerability   Page 15

#3 Crossroads   Page 22

#4 Age - Old Story of the Hatfield's and McCoy's   Page 27

#5 What Insanity Looks Like   Page 31

#6 Inner Knowing   Page 41

#7 The Meaningful Unsung Heroes   Page 50

     Today's Battles, Tomorrow's Strength

#8 All Trials & Tribulations Have Value   Page 72

     Tribulation is the Divine Medicine

#9 The Natural Beauty of Spirals   Page 86

     A fervent Prayer

#10 If It Is Important to You-You Will Find a Way   Page 98

#11 A Picture is Worth a 1000 Words   Page 113

     Painting the Beauty of Heaven and Earth

     Through My Vision

     Inside the Artist's Studio

#12 Creating a New Treasure Map for the Future   Page 126

     From Outward Appearance to Inner Substance

#13 Natural Solutions – What is Reiki   Page 137

     Experience the Power of Unseen Energy

#14 Rainbows Exist in Everyone   Page 143

     Get to Know Your Vibes through Auras and Chakras

#15 Life Path Is About Seeing God in Everything   Page 151

#16 Everyone Leaves a Legacy   Page 159

About the Author   Page 166

Glossary   Page 168

Acknowledgements

There are not enough words in the English language to acknowledge a true earth angel. Ailill's husband John Star has tirelessly and lovingly been her primary care giver, companion, coach, spiritual advisor, housekeeper, gardener and cook.

How could she add any real meaning by just saying, "Thank you?" Maya Angelou once said, "People will forget what you said, people will forget what you did, but people will never forget how you made them feel.

John showed her and allowed her to feel it was an honor and privilege to take care of her. That was a challenging task because Ailill is so fiercely independent and has never had to depend on anyone before and she resisted every inch of the way. He would laughingly tease her about how she was gradually progressing in accepting his help and care when she finally allowed him to do the laundry.

Ailill is such a perfectionist in most areas of her life which added a tremendous burden on him. They cried together many times when her health crisis appeared to put her on the brink of death. Through his own pain, grief and courage he continually supported her wishes even when she quit her medications and openly discussed and signed advanced directives with Hospice to not have CPR due to being an imminent stroke and heart attack risk. He sat in conferences with her health care professionals and listened to how he is not to do anything when the time comes. His valor and commitment to her has been an experience I can't begin to describe. Ailill is so blessed to have this earth angel in her life.

Ailill acknowledges that every human being doing life is a unique one of kind creation. Great thinkers who have gone before us say it this way:

"Today you are you, that is truer than true. There is no one alive who is Youer than you."
~Dr. Seuss

"To be yourself in a world that is constantly trying to make you something else is the greatest accomplishment."
~Ralph Waldo Emerson

Winter Reflections

Mikki Alhart Artist/Author

I gratefully acknowledge the publication of Hay House as follows: For consideration which I, Mikki Alhart, (hereinafter called the "Grantor"), irrevocably grant to Hay House, Inc.(hereinafter called the "Publisher") a non-exclusive, perpetual, worldwide license to reproduce and publish the following Material, in whole or in part of, or as embodied in, EARTHMAGIC ORACLE CARDS, by Steven D. Farmer, for publication by Publisher (hereinafter called the "Work").

WINTER SOLSTICE By Steven D. Farmer Hay House

Winter Reflections

"This midpoint of winter is not only the shortest day of the year, but also the longest night. The world is very still and the land dormant. Various "festivals of light" are celebrated, and have been for thousands of years, serving as a reminder that the light will indeed return. Throughout many cultures there are tales describing this time as the birth of the archetypal Sun King- including the Christian story of Jesus' birth-representing the hope of renewal from the darkest period of the solar cycle. This image portrays a simple yet powerful representation of the winter solstice. We see a clear reflection of the snowy woods on the still, frozen waters of the lake. The blue tint drapes the scene with an even greater sense of quiet and solace, inviting us to walk very softly lest we disturb the intense yet gentle grace of this scene. The reflection of the trees on the frozen lake reminds us that this is a time for us to go inside-to both our physical shelter as well as our internal world-and there contemplate the season that has passed, the season that is, and the seasons yet to come.

Review the past year and ask yourself what the most important lessons you have had to learn are, what you have accomplished, and what dreams and visions you want to manifest in the upcoming year. Whether it has been a relatively smooth ride or a challenging series of events, acknowledge your experience as being the work of Source, no matter what your judgments, fears, or joys are. Honor whatever has happened over the previous several months with gratitude and forgiveness. Then let it go. Allow yourself some solitude so you can spend some quiet, slow time in reflection".

Once you feel complete, reflect on your present .life, especially focusing on what you are grateful for. When you are finished, consider what is to come-all the different possibilities and potential that exists before you. Allow your imagination to roam without limitation or ambition, and see what shows up. Notice how you feel in your body with whatever scenario plays out in your mind. These are previews of that which is gestating, and can manifest and grow when cared for properly. Patience and stillness is called for here, for just as the Earth cycles have their own pace, so does this cycle.

IN GOD'S WAITING ROOM
The Diary of Ailill O'Sullivan

Introduction

"Dying is a wild night and a new road." ~ Emily Dickinson

In bed for 12 months, being told Hospice is her next step Ailill wrote in her journal in an attempt to say goodbye to versions of herself that could no longer exist in the world. Ailill reflected on her birth name pronounced (all-ell) which meant sprite or other-worldly being. Her whole life was a true reflection of experiences that only validated she did not belong on this planet. Only now being on her death bed did her factual vision clear enough to allow her to honestly see herself for the first time?

Ailill was 5' 10" tall since she was twelve years old and wore a C cup. She had beautiful blonde hair and an extraordinarily large personality. In eighth grade her prophecy was announced on stage that she was going to be Jane Mansfield's double. At home she was called Baby Huey, Amazon, Goody Two-Shoes and Miss Van Aster. Looking back now Ailill realized all the mixed messages she received growing up was what made her feel alien and insignificant most of her life. Ailill was normally hyper-active, a mover and a shaker. If she couldn't be a human-doing at break neck speed how was she going to transition to just being a human beached whale?

She spent her time re-reading her past journals and contemplated her life story with all the hidden secrets poured out on the pages of her diaries. She struggled with the issues of revealing secrets and wondered how she was going to tell her own powerful and sometimes shameful truths. Ailill reflected on how everyone is equally ashamed of their successes by not talking about them for fear of being thought of as egotistical or prideful. She secretly wrote about her spirituality in those journals because her family referred to her as their wo-woo mother, grandmother and yes, even now, great grandmother.

4

Ailill wrote in her diary; "Anyone doing life today will personally relate when looking at the big questions of life. Why did this happen? How could it have happened? Where is justice and fairness? What still makes sense? What paths lead to healing and how to deal with timeless questions?" She was amazed at how humor and fortitude allowed her family to turn their scars into stars.

This event wasn't her first tragedy: two daughters died of cancer, her brother died last month, her husband died of an accidental overdose at age 52 after years in recovery, and her adult children hated and blamed her because she was their alcoholic mother. Ailill's diary was to become the private saga of a wildly passionate woman who needed to tell her true story. She will introduce you to the people who bonded in sorrow and those who carried their hatred for decades. Thirty-three years of being a recovering alcoholic did not minimize the wreckage of her past.

Ailill was forced to stop and look at the great power her secrets had over her and how diminished she had become. She recognized that as she wrote about the five generations of the O'Sullivan clan that they all had become co-conspirators of the family dynamics they didn't agree with and wanted to break away from. She wrote about the good and bad secrets that held a great power over many of the family members. She was caught in a conflict to speak or not to speak. To remain closed and complicit, or to open up and take the risk of losing friends and family being shamed once again into submission. She knew these conflicts haunt people all their lives, solidifying the silence. She had to discover a way out of her own trap, release her past and write the truth. In the quiet of God's waiting room she had to become clear about the program that lived in her head.

As Ailill wrote about the Legacy of the O'Sullivan clan she realized that family members will laugh, cry and get angry. She was determined to be open about all of it and hopefully that would allow everyone to feel safe talking about it. In looking at her own mortality, saying good-bye, she created a space for a different version of herself which in turn allowed for her personal journey to emerge. Staring death squarely in the face she discovered that she had a new choice; a new understanding that she was the only one who could live the remainder of her best life now. It is in the now moment of this process, saying yes to more good times that she acknowledged to herself that she did have the gift of insight as an 'ole crone' who can see the losses, tragedies and heartbreaks as detours and the building blocks of soul growth and stamina.

Ailill re-read a lifetime of entries in her journals and diaries containing all of her inspirations, prayers and challenges. Privately she risked exposing her eccentric, passionate imagination, grief, humor and creativity. She intuitively knew that all of us are more alike than different and her reverent hope was that everyone would see themselves in the mirror.

The stories of Ailill O'Sullivan will reach far beyond the personal, her memoirs pose larger questions about the nature of our identity and what it means to rebuild in the aftermath of betrayal. When looking at the end of life, it doesn't have to mean giving up hope, but rather reframing what to hope for. Ailill's diary speaks to the humanness in all of us.

IN GOD'S WAITING ROOM
Forward

Life Lessons of an Old Woman
Turning Our Scars into Stars

Oh my God, I got the chills so many times towards the end of reading Ailill's diary. I realized that it was in the beginning that she was sharing her ending. Apropos don't you think? Reading her messages from God's Waiting Room was not just about her or them but without distinction included everyone and everybody. Each story was above any culture or time period that represented the best in terms of life lessons and timeless wisdom. From the perspective of her 'Old Crone Self,' she embodied instinctive ways of channeling wisdom, inner knowing, and intuitions as she recognized the guidance she received in the transitions of all life. This book is a gift to everybody who is doing life. In Ailill's old age she discovered how each of us is a knower of mysteries who can shine their own light of wisdom as the "Way Shower" in the creation of our personal stories.

Reading Ailill O'Sullivan's personal diary I had to share her legacy. You will discover through her memoirs and journal entries the incredible story spanning five generations of the heroic travels and experiences of the O'Sullivan Clan and all the characters that participated in her life story, I am confident that everyone will relate to the real-life saga through the characters and experiences of her stories.

It is through our personal stories and struggles that we create a legacy that fosters wonderful, intelligent passionate people to choose their paths. This is a story about all of us.

Each one of you will see yourselves in the mirror because we do live not only separate lives but inside one another. Your image in the mirror is the legacies you will create through your connection to your personal families and life narrative. The fictional characters are the reference point to illustrate the multigenerational patterns of how we stay as sick as our secrets. The chapters and stories will identify our humanness and how we are all much more alike than different. In sharing Ailill's diary I intend that all of us see and recognize how loved and cherished we truly are to one another even when we don't know how to show it, let alone say it.

Ailill's journaling openly shared her naked vulnerability of how her life read like she did everything wrong but ended upright. Exceedingly right, beyond her imagination of a life fully lived with no regrets. You will read about a journey viewed from a speeding runaway train, from the vantage point of an old lady who was literally stopped in her tracks. Ailill kept a journal for years and she lived 1,000 times over. In the end she realized she was truly lucky to have walked in her shoes even with, all of her so-called missteps.

Ailill was not sure how long she would live when she wrote her diary but she did discover the privilege of wanting to share her life lessons. She decided she wanted to continue to learn until her last breath. How many of us can say they graduated hospice? The last year in bed with the privacy of her diary she discovered the inspiration to share openly her life review. Ailill looked at her life, her loves, her losses, her pain, her dreams, her achievements, her happiness, and all the lessons that embodied these points of reference.

She hoped that just because she lived her entire life on the default settings, that others would gain inspiration for how they can customize the way they live. In-between is where passions are realized, love is found, strength is gained, and priceless life-long memories are made. She wrote about the willingness she discovered in embracing total gratification. When she had to stop and look at death in the face she saw that it is the small, incremental changes that always change everything in the long run.

Ailill's disappointments in life were often the result of misplaced expectations. Not being "OK" all the time is normal. Sensitivity can be a superpower. She could now see how she was ashamed of her feelings. It took her losing everything; by being sick in bed for twelve months to realize that most of the time she never learned how to be happy needing more, because she needed less. Ailill wrote, "Those whom we choose to spend time with matters immensely. I didn't learn to say "No", because I was a chronic people pleaser." The sad fact is it left no time for the really important people in her life. Relationship boundaries are lifesavers.

Make it happen before it's too late. Ailill realized as she faced the last chapter, she could see the true colors of the people who said they cared about her. She learned that the people who left her gave her room to grow in the space they abandoned. Don't give part-time people full-time attention.

As long as you are truly the best you can be, it will show. Look on the sunny side of everything and make your optimism come true.

What Ailill Learned the Hard Way - Choose to Hear the Angel That Lives on Your Shoulder.

Ailill believed in eternity and knew that her voice may be the whispers in the ears of her loved ones someday?

Ailill's last entry in her diary, "To all who read this I leave you with; Think well of yourself and proclaim this fact to the world out loud, not in words, but with great deeds. Many of my loved ones say they don't know me because of my busyness of the obsession of trying to improve myself which caused me to think I missed the mark of being there for them."

"I can choose to learn my lessons through hard knocks and opposites or practice positive thinking to attract the highest best the world has to offer."

"Live in faith that the whole world is on your side so long as you are true to the best that is in you."

Chapter 1

In God's Waiting Room

Is the beginning the end or is it simply a new beginning?

Most stories begin with Once Upon a time or in the beginning. This story is about Ailill O'Sullivan's ending, with full knowledge that her time in God's Waiting Room will occur only once upon her time. The title of her story in God's Waiting Room was coined by her then nineteen year old grandson, who said; "Grandma is in God's waiting room."

Ailill's original intention was to write a letter to each one of her ten grandchildren, two great grandchildren, brother and sisters and her son and daughters. She shared with her husband that once she had completed this task she wanted him to give each one of them a letter after her death. His response was;"Why wait?" Consequently, she decided not to wait. What she discovered as she began to draft her message to each one individually that much of what she wanted to share would have to be repeated numerous times so she decided to put it into a narrative so that each one could meet the other one through her eyes, heart, love and perspective. Many of her family members have been estranged from one another throughout the years.

I was intrigued in reading Ailill's diary how she intermingled her present day experiences along with her memories of the past. She had to call her twenty-eight year old granddaughter, Makenna, and let her know that there was no way she could physically attend her wedding. Makenna was so surprised; she didn't even know that her grandmother was sick. That's when Ailill realized she had hidden herself away for the last thirteen months from everybody, almost. The truth is that when she realized she was facing the end; everything that wasn't real was stripped away. She wanted to become the most real person that she would ever be. She knew it was time to be more real than she had ever been before. The ambulance ride, hospital stay, coming home to Palliative care and then given instructions on how the next step was Hospice, she had spent a year in bed almost full time writing, reading, praying and meditating. Her home nurses, primary care doctor, cardiologist, pulmonologist, endocrinologist and physical therapist had all agreed with her hospice nurse, that she was just a Hot Mess. Ailill put on such a happy face and strong front that she was accused of having a death wish or that she was being stoic. She had to look up the definition of stoic and agreed that the definition fit: (a person who can endure pain or hardship without showing their feelings or complaining). In fairness to her though, how could she tell people, "Oh by the way, I have been given multiple diagnoses of diabetes, hypertension (blood pressure 210/110), late stage COPD, chronic bowel obstruction, heart palpitations and on top of all that I am deathly allergic to all my pharmaceuticals." Medical procedures and surgeries are out of the question because as she had been told she would not survive. In her mind, she was never going to get old and the only thing she had to talk about was her aliments. One more time, she realized never say never because you may get to experience it. The result being she couldn't talk about it because for the last year that has been the main focus.

Ailill was known as a manically active person all her life. 'Run harder, go faster and do more,' had been her internal mantra for 72 years. She had been accused of being an over achiever, perfectionist, intense personality, overly passionate and a mover and a shaker. Apparently these are true labels as her entire family; children and grandchildren shared this common characteristic. Mentors had invited her to hang up her super-women suit but that was no longer an issue as it had obviously disintegrated. This is the core of the message she wanted to share with all her loved ones and friends before the universe took away her roller skates. She missed so much by going, doing, accomplishing and striving that she missed the beautiful scenery along the way. It has taken the supreme challenge of the dying process to give Ailill the courage to show everyone the truth of who she really is.

No one wants to talk about dying but she had to. Death is hard work! Death is in control of the process. She realized she could not influence its course. She realized now what a controller she was her entire life. All she could do is wait. She was given her life, she had to live it, and now she was giving it back. Ailill lovingly thanked everyone of who will be reading her words because she was approaching death.

Understand that she found writing her Life-Review helped her validate her whole life journey. She knew she was beginning at the end and traveling backwards. Writing in her diary she discovered her unprotected naked truth. Her spiritual and religious beliefs were her foundation and the solace that comes from that. There was so much left unsaid that she wanted to share with all of her family and friends.

Please know this is not her last will and testament as she knows she will be forever with you. Do you know how long eternity is? Death is both inevitable and uncertain. We all know it will happen, but we don't know when. Each of us is dying to get out of here. She is looking forward to her next great adventure which, she believes is back home with her creator who she calls God. She discovered our human body, our whole existence, is extremely fragile. The intensity of her spiritual practice has trained her mind to accept that as truth instead of being in denial. Ailill knew we are truly spiritual beings, born in His image on a journey through Earth school. I found her writings to be giddy and whimsical as if she wrote these words and for the first time she didn't have to censor them or worry whether others would agree or disagree. It's such a great gift to own truth and say it out loud and let it be what it is. This new found freedom is almost incomprehensible. Gandhi said: "Live as if you were to die tomorrow. Learn as if you live forever."

I am so glad that I have a chance to write and share her diary. She didn't always live the way she wanted to be remembered but now she can pen her own obituary and ask you to remember that her actions were that of a child of God, just like you and me. Even now she knew that God wasn't finished with her yet and she would never go to the head of the class or graduate this thing called eternal life. Don't misunderstand her because she knew that if she gave you a full laundry list of her failures and character defects as a wife, mother, daughter, grandmother, great grandmother, sister and friend it would be a novel unto itself of her personal shortcomings and failures. She became fully aware that she lived in a dual universe as she learned most of her valuable lessons through opposites.

Psalms 37:25 (KJV)
I have been young, and now am old; yet have I not seen the righteous forsaken, nor His seed begging bread.

Ailill wrote about imagining living in a perfect universe. She would love to share in one line how she made this world a better place to live in. She wasn't sure she could answer that, because as she looked in the mirror, took a microscope to her heart, and asked herself "Who is the Real Me, Unfiltered?" She saw her masks, her costumes, her job titles and roles she had played. She had the opportunity to sojourn through all the personal journals she had written and still looked for her true essence in search of what had made her unique. She discovered, in asking these questions of herself, it took her to a place of being surreal. The reason for this is because of her role as a counselor, healer, and teacher she was always able to see the true essence of everyone else. She had 20/20 vision when it came to seeing others in her life because she was such a strong empath. She sometimes did not know where you begin and she left off because she could honestly feel you. She would always share with people that her wish for them is that they could see themselves through her eyes, wonderfully divine, precious, and unique souls. She has been given a special blessing. Knowing that in a million years forwards and backwards there can be only one of you or me no matter our faith or beliefs. All her life she prayed for inverted eyesight so she could see herself clearly just once. Maybe that is what makes her unique. She always taught passionately, that what she taught is what she needed to learn herself. She believed that is what made her such a good teacher. She believed in being the teacher, do as I say, not as I do.

Ailill O'Sullivan intended to write personal and special messages to the people who she thought would remember her. At first she thought this would be a very easy task, but in retrospect, she realized that it wasn't about the people that she wished would miss her but in fact about the people who she thought she meant something special to. As she mentally went over her list of how she thought others would remember she found her costumes to be numerous and diversified. If truly we are as Shakespeare said, "All the world's a stage, and all the men and women merely players: they have their exits and their entrances; and one man in his time plays many parts, his acts being seven ages." She couldn't believe all the roles she had played. I will discuss this in future chapters because as she jokingly shared; "If I was ever to write an overview of my life no one would believe it." The truth of the matter is that it does read like a fiction because she has lived a minimum of six lives in this one. The upside of that statement is that in this glorious experience of her life, no grass ever had a chance to grow under her feet. Ailill's epitaph might read that she left no stone unturned. She strived to learn from her tragedies as well as her successes and everything in between. Her intentions are that each of us will see and feel our own soulful truth. It's not just a cliché to say that there are positively absolutely no mistakes in God's world, and she proved it over and over again to herself. When we make good choices good things happened when we make bad choices bad things happened. Another important lesson that Ailill learned is it really isn't good or bad a right or wrong it's only our perspectives that made it so.

At the time of this writing the first chapters of her thoughts are about her ending. You will see the courage it took for her to go forward from this point on in sharing her personal journal during this last rite of passage. Because it was her heart's desire to give her loved ones an understanding why in saying yes to every distraction, temptation and possibility, (because she didn't know how to say no) she inadvertently derailed the goals she set for herself. Her goal being; she wanted to love, nourish and protect her loved ones with everything that she was. The only thing she was sorry about is that she didn't know how to love each one better.

As I share her inner most thoughts and prayers from her personal journals, I believe that what I'm writing now will evolve in giving everyone some insight as to her last paragraph. She was still searching her soul for those words, one paragraph, which might be said of her by someone after she has departed.

Ailill came full circle now that had completed her life story. She recognized now why she couldn't heal because she kept pretending she wasn't hurt. Her diary read, "If you remember anything of me after I leave this world, remember I loved even when foolish; that I cared even when it was unwanted. When my physical body is gone my prayer is that you remember my heart."

14

Chapter 2

VUNERABILITY

"Vulnerability is the birthplace of innovation, creativity and change" ~ Dr. Brene' Brown

Being told you are going to die was, in her mind, a mistake. Ailill just could not wrap her head around the concept. It was illogical to her because she was still living. She needed to process this information and understand what this meant to her. She asked herself, "How do I live when every day my illness brought such physical suffering?" She was emotionally challenged and every day it seemed as though she was being exposed to the truth that her life, as she knew it, was coming to an end, according to all of her doctors and caregivers, who kept trying to get her to go to the hospital to do this dying because it was to be an imminent event. She vehemently refused to participate even though she felt like just giving in and giving up.

Ailill had to dig deep into her heart of hearts to make way into her soul by sifting through all the voices of fear, loss, anger, and regrets. She realized that what was needed was a complete life review. She poured her feelings into her journal. She wrote for days on end. She discovered the unexplored work she still had to do in her relationships. I discuss this part of her review in the chapter entitled All Trials and Tribulations Have Value.

Ailill realized we all do amazing things when we have to. With her life in the balance, she thought maybe she could bring her highest and best good to this experience called dying, after all, she wasn't dead yet. She thought there had to be a way for her to find some good in this awful scary diagnosis.

She had to move away from the conditioned mindset that because someone says you are dying, it doesn't mean you have to surrender yourself to the experience by lying down and waiting for it to happen. Her inner search began to look and feel like she was becoming a narcissist. She had lost so much by being confined to her bed that she realized she was already believing in and grieving her demise.

Ailill was very familiar with the process of grief as she had experienced it so many times during her life. Grief always felt so self-centered to her. Her inner voices cried out, "Oh poor me, look at what I've lost." Her ego was loud with voices of incredulity and at the same time incorrigibility. She felt like nothing but a beached whale, unable to do anything about the way she looked because she literally had no energy. She chided herself for what she saw as her excessive need for admiration and acceptance. Then the big debate committee would convene in her head. She encountered the war of self-doubt; "What if I missed the boat? What if everything I believe in was nothing more than someone else's ideas? What if I didn't just make mistakes, but blew it on this particular journey?" It was through this rite of passage or the dark night of the soul playing out in her mind that she concluded that no matter what it looked like; her life truly was the purest version of itself. She believed that everything happens in Divine order.

She wanted so much to get better but if it didn't happen for her it just had to be OK. She realized it was she, who was blocking any blessings she might find within this journey by giving the naysayer in her head way too much attention as she struggled to walk her talk. Her belief system was strong and she knew this was the ultimate moment when she needed to put on her big girl panties and step up to the plate she was being served.

Then something happened during her morning meditation. She felt like she was broken wide open. There was nothing to hide and nothing to be ashamed of. There was nothing but the light and she met and experienced Jesus in person. He was everything she had imagined in her prayers and mediations, but his persona was so much more that she was lost for words. All the teachings she had learned as a child came flooding back into her memory. She heard these words:

Ezekiel 36:26 (KJV)
"A new heart also will I give you, and a new spirit will I put within you: and I will take away the stony heart out of your flesh, and I will give you a heart of flesh."

16

Ephesians 4:25 (KJV)
"Therefore each of you must put off falsehood and speak truthfully to your neighbor, for we are all one."

Of course, Jesus didn't quote Ezekiel or Ephesians to her; she had heard these words before and had to look them up. What this validated for her was her belief in a Universe of Divine Order. This principle illustrates that the basic premise of all the major religions teaches us that we are all part of a single plan directed by the same God. It is the core of all spiritual truths; the unity of God is the unity of humanity.

Reading the volumes written in Ailill's journals and the diary was like attending one of her classes. She was such a passionate teacher, counselor and student of life. She wrote inspirational messages to herself throughout her convalescence. Every religion proclaims that there is but one religion which is progressively revealed by God through His prophets and messengers. As humanity matures, our capacity for understanding and the desire for enlightenment also grow. The outward differences between religions, what their texts subscribe to, might be due to the exigencies of the time and place or the era in which the religion was born.

Ancient texts proclaim that the essential nature of the messenger is twofold: they are at once human and divine. They are divine in that they all come from the same God and expound his teachings. In this light, they are seen as the same, and yet, they are separate and individual, known by different names. Each fulfills a definite mission and is entrusted with a particular revelation.

Her research over the last fifty years had proven to her that the truth is the truth no matter where it comes from. We are all one with the divine educators, master teachers, and human/God: which include Krishna, Jesus, Buddha, Muhammad, and many others.

She owned this truth and felt she must include it in her diary as part of her departing gift, sort of a blatant exposure of her innermost self. Being transparent meant allowing herself to be vulnerable. She hadn't always openly shared her deep beliefs with some of her friends, family or relatives. She was afraid some would consider this blasphemy, and besides, what if she was

17

wrong? She hid her feelings and opinions because she wanted to be included in all of those circles and didn't want to feel like an outcast. She chose to share this secret with her diary and now and it gives me great pleasure to be her voice and help her finally speak her truth.

Ailill believed in the Universal Christ as One God. Her husband, John Star, is a member of the Church of Christ and has been for most of his life. His family was ultra-conservative and devoutly Christian; it is how he identifies with his heritage. He is strong in his beliefs and is totally committed. Ailill and her husband couldn't be more diversified but they have learned from each other. They honor each other's path without the need to convert, explain or coheres each other. They proved that by lovingly embracing such different belief systems, anyone can do the same.

Imagine a new earth with no more wars in the name of religion, no more discrimination about whose God is superior, in other words, no more compare and compete. We could agree to understand that no one needs to be the best or have the most. The only thing we would lose is our belief in our insufficiencies. Scarcity and fear would dissipate under the weight of a bigger understanding of Love in God's point of view.

The freedom she gained in understanding her need to be accepted is humorous on some weird level. She confessed that she tip-toed around all the important issues; like religion, and needing to be accepted by her family. This, in turn, allowed doubt and fear to rule her actions. It took looking at the possibility of her death in the face and standing strong in front of the fear that was pressing in on her to proclaim to her world:
"It is Life and it is My Life Now".

Her naked vulnerability is just as sacred to her now as it was in spending a lifetime of trying to be good enough to earn God's Love. Broken dreams and broken promises now looked like detours instead of failures. While she was still in God's waiting room she was sharing her journey as it was unfolding for her in the present moment. Ailill was sure that her life would continue to unfold in the next dimension as she was positive she would continue perfecting her existence. She didn't see heaven as a rest stop but as a continuation of the desire to exist in the image of her creator. She fully hoped and planned to be of service in the next realm.

Realizing she didn't have to live up to her expectations of the purest version of herself was such a tremendous relief. By acknowledging her character defects and shadow side she inadvertently lost all resistance. Resistance was her obstacle; she thought she had the power and the faith and the stamina to make it all turn out differently. Her resistance is what kept the negative mind-set alive in her overachieving efforts. Resistance was the fuel for her doubt and fear. To keep her resistance alive she had to compare and compete. She did not manifest her best intentions but instead, she realized she just gave lip service to her little self and her little ego-mind kept the lie alive. The focus was on what was wrong while ignoring what was right and the possibilities that might be presented in the surrendering to what was happening to her.

Her journaling presented a new question: "What if all my needs and wants were met?" If she understood that to be true then she realized she had a brief glimpse into how mystics and sages knew that every minute of life, every moment in time is a miracle. This journey into this near-death experience was about giving up who she needed to be, just being who she was and the astonishment of who/what she was becoming. What a flash of insight, she suddenly remembered the saying that none of us came here with an owner's manual. Since you can't take it with you, she couldn't have a U-Haul behind her hearse, so what could she leave behind but her legacy. She came here alone and she would leave alone. Her resolution was the solution. She told herself: "I can have and be a bigger me. I need to sincerely embrace this idea and walk in the direction of my potential."

Acknowledging that she was nothing more than energy she decided to line up with her vibration, believing that what she came here with is exactly what she will leave here with. She had proven for herself that negative thinking and actions lowered her vibration, but she needed to re-think that concept as well because everything is just an idea in the mind of the thinker. She challenged herself to just be with her vibration without censor or expectations. Immediately she had a revelation that she came to understand that she could not have what she was unwilling to become. Guess what happened next? Ailill began to show up as herself. She could lose herself when she was by herself. Everything else was just signposts along the way.

She went to a place of thinking more independently than she ever had before. When she thought of all the circumstances in her life she only saw her choices. She didn't always choose love when presented with the face of hate. She didn't always choose seeing the rainbows in the storms. The ultimate vision of her soul was that she was part of the source and that source was within her. Words are completely insufficient and what she was feeling at that moment was beyond anyone's imagination or fantasy. Ailill was feeling, seeing and understanding her beautiful uniqueness. She was part of a bigger vibration that existed as a true channel which allowed her to experience the presence of God. She understood what it meant when people talked about nirvana, the void that is everything and nothing at the same time. This void was total bliss, beyond words or explanation. Her life belonged to God. Her life is God's life.

Ailill had an aura and chakra business she called, 'Your 'DNA in Color'. Our genetic connection encompasses all of our ancestors. God is always Godding through each of us. Every night as she prayed to admonish all her losses, tragedies and victories there were moments when the real Soul of a soul could only be discovered away from all the noise. The sacred does show its face in the most unexpected places. Now, fully embracing what some might call the darkness, she continued to examine every one of her daily experiences because she was aware that if she continued to close her eyes to what she was doing she would remain in the dark and that is the place of the unknown.

Every day, she asked herself, "What is giving me life today?" She examined and embraced her pity parties, having to suffer, being sick for so long. She embraced her fear of the unknown and was able to cherish her sacred moments with the highest of all, the original vibration which is God.

Being human, when we can't be productive is a fine gift in humility which allows us to remain teachable. It all boils down to, "It is what it is". Ailill worked hard during her isolation. She answered her own questions about what she might be avoiding now and what

20

situation or circumstances she had avoided throughout her life. She didn't shy away from the hard truths. Working in the quiet of her isolated state she realized how hard it is to face all the goodbyes while keeping the anticipation or the wonderment of a child in her heart for what new adventure awaited her.

Spirit speaks to us in our language. Releasing all judgment she now had time to pay attention to her own life. No longer did she have to worry about how others might need to agree with what was happening to her.

Validating her desires to fulfill her destiny, her true life's purpose is in and of itself the recognition of the life force she was blessed with. Yes, her soul displayed the fingerprints of God and any of the deep scars from her experiences only came about to enable her to witness the Sacred in her life. The good and the bad canceled each other out. In the wake of all of this is enlightenment and truth. It never was an either/or proposition. It was always about beauty and goodness. It was her greatest struggles, which forced her to her knees and allowed Ailill to know God on a personal level.

We are all desperately trying to learn, in an era of crisis and chaos, to embrace the divine on our path. Our trials reverberate as vibrations that show up in each of our lives, our families and our communities. We are a global family. We are all affected by the vibrations of chaos and despair. The good news is that we are equally affected by vibrations of acceptance, joy and love.

After all this extensive soul searching and learning to honor her truth, in the end, she wrote: "Yes, I may have done a lot of things wrong in my life. The little me could never measure up to my perfectionist's expectations but, the bigger me, that part of me which abides in God's Grace, that part of me that is I AM, is alive and well. Thank you, GOD."

Chapter 3

Crossroads

*"One of the hardest decisions you'll ever face in life is
Choosing whether to walk away or try harder."* Unknown

We all go through so many changes during our lifetime and some
of those changes are lovingly referred to as rites of passage. This
book is nothing less than Ailill O'Sullivan's personal rite of
passage. I have written it all down with the full knowledge that her
visions are that of a seventy-two-year-old seasoned grandmother
who originally wrote it all down from years of her journaling and
study. She honestly was able to access how foggy her inner vision
was because of her blocked feelings through much of her life path.
Don't be surprised if you are able at this juncture of her life to see
the humor in some of her horrific tragedies and how she makes
light of some of the experiences that seemed so difficult and dark
at the time. The heritage of her family is one of heroes and
survivors who have turned, and still are in the process of turning
scars into stars.

Ailill wrote about a worshipful wish she carried in her heart. She
so wanted to share her hard-won wisdom with each of her
grandchildren, great-grandchildren and adult children sitting in her
lap while she hugged and kissed each one over and over. She so
wanted to let them know who she was, who their ancestors were
and how deeply meaningful they were to her. The consequence of
this is that at this point in her life she felt totally estranged from the
people she loved most in this world. Hopefully, by sharing her
memoirs each of her loved ones will discover 25 or more things
they never knew about her. My wish is that they will come to
realize just how deeply she loved each and every one of them. I
have written it all down with full knowledge that she is soon to be
their late ancestor, so please indulge me as I take you on a trip
down memory lane that was gleaned from her diary.

As all of us know we all have many lives in this one lifetime. The
young child, adolescent, student, parent, and grandparents still live
(or will live) inside of each of us. I have come to understand what
Ailill's visions were. Even though she was raised in the same

family and they may have been at the same place at the same time, she discovered contradictions of the same experiences. She understood that each one will see through their own eyes and their own understanding. The story of the elephant that lives in our living room is so true. Everyone touches it, knows it is there but no one talks about it. I bring this up because Ailill has a reputation for her stories. She tends to embellish, exaggerate and add to her story not only in her writing but to herself. She admits that fantasy thinking; to this day, sometimes made life much more tolerable and funny. She maximized this coping skill by telling herself, "I am Ailill O'Sullivan and I am a descendant of the blarney stone.

Her daughter, Brianna Teagan discovered by sharing their joint memories that they just didn't match. Brianna lovingly explained to her mother that one of the main reasons she actively disliked her while growing up, was in fact, her expectations of who and what a mother should be and she didn't live up to her expectations. They mutually agreed that the truth is we all make it up as we go along. There is your truth and my truth so the challenge then becomes to agree to disagree. Understand please, I am not defending Ailill's position as a good mother. She knew she made choices that hurt her family and loved ones in multiple ways. She fell below her own moral compass due to the progression of her alcoholism. She was not justifying or minimizing her part in the role she played in the life of her loved ones. She truly understood more than ever before how accountable she was for her actions. I hope you will understand this more as her story unfolds.

As Ailill looked back on her childhood, she wrote about how her story had evolved over the years. This is natural as it comes with maturity. She was the eldest of four siblings and she openly admitted how her story continued to change over the years. Her childhood experience was fraught with challenges, sorrow and lots of fear. For many years her victim story could bring tears to the most insensitive among us. As she reviewed her years of journaling she happily acknowledged that she had outgrown her need for pity parties and blaming other people, places and things as an excuse for being who she was. She used character assassination to ridicule her family, especially her own mother. What she didn't pay attention to was the example she exhibited concerning how to be in the world depicting a mother-daughter relationship. Her daughters were definitely taking notes. Thusly they pulled no punches in letting her know just how much they hated her over the years.

Her parents were hard-working blue-collar workers who firmly believed in family. Her mother plainly expressed, openly letting her know how much she didn't like her. Her father was her hero even though he was a jolly periodic alcoholic. Mom was the strict disciplinarian of the family, and she could wield her authority and venom in the blink of an eye. She provided wonderful meals, made their clothes and worked hard all of her life. This was the only way she knew how to show her love. Ailill eventually came to understand that this was because her mother could not possibly give something she never had. Ailill can't remember her parents ever saying they loved her and she felt she worked tirelessly to get their approval.

Her grandmother died when her mother was a baby and her father worked on the road crews in Oregon so he was never around. Her grandfather begged and pleaded for anyone who could take her mother in, so she went from place to place, never experiencing a safe, loving and secure environment. Ailill felt that she had received a valuable gift which allowed her to be able to share her story with other abused, abandoned and frightened people. This was her tried and true lesson because the experience brought about true knowledge.

Forgiveness comes from understanding that the people who were supposed to love us just didn't know-how. Ailill confessed she carried this generational legacy into the raising of her own three children. She made everything look really good on the outside while they all withered from lack of attention, recognition, and love. She always knew somewhere deep inside herself that she lacked the ability to truly bond with her children as well as she was able to bond with her husband's but she remained in the dark as to why she was like she was.

Her father left home at age fourteen after a brutal fight with her grandfather. He was trying to protect his mother from another beating. Her father, Maddox O'Sullivan was estranged from his family. He lived on his own since the age of fourteen. Grandfather O'Sullivan was a physically abusive raging alcoholic. She wrote about this because she had lived long enough now to realize that her father had his own issues but physical abuse and being cold of heart was not one of them. In reviewing her life she became aware that each generation was evolving to a more loving, compassionate and supportive family despite the last four generations.

Grandfather Murphy came to America from Ireland when he was only twenty-one years old. Her story about her grandfather read like the movie The Gangs of New York. His story is one of discrimination and it is heartbreaking. A very vivid memory Ailill had about her grandfather's funeral, was when she was only six years old and the casket was in the living room with a black cloth covering it. She did not understand what an Irish wake was and why everyone was drinking, laughing and dancing. She wondered, "Why everyone was so happy that her grandfather died".

Neither her children, grandchildren or great-grandchildren had never asked about their heritage but she knew the day would come when their curiosity about their DNA would someday surface. She did a workup in Ancestry.com and 23 and me because science has now proven that even our cells have memory. Our genetic predisposition is no longer a theory but a fact of life. It is a blueprint of our intended destiny and influences us in ways we are just beginning to understand. Our heritage is linked to everyone as she believed we are all one with our creator, who she called God. Ailill wrote to herself numerous times about her firm understanding that God is Godding through each of us and everyone else. Each of us is a special one of a kind expression of His Grace and image.

Her great grandmother, on her mother's side, Tuukka Norse, arrived by boat from Finland when she was very young. Ailill was named after her grandmother, who was always known as Ailill, not Tuukka (pronounced TU-Kah) as it was a popular name in Finland. She admitted to being very sensitive about the immigrant issues in our country today. She was only two generations removed and she realized that none of her family would even be here if it wasn't for her ancestor's courage to seek a better life. They also felt they would be welcomed to the United States and believed their lives would be more prosperous.

The Finnish clan settled in Donley Idaho, which is still to this day known as Finn Valley. She often visited her cousins and their families in Donley and she was taken to her grandparent's original settlement and gravesite. They had dug a sauna in a hillside and loved to sweat and then roll in the snow.

It was in the 1980s when she was around forty years old that they were invited to a pot luck at Aunt Sima and Uncle Fat's church (he was always skinny and she had no idea why he had that nickname). Ailill was overwhelmed by the resemblance she had with her Finnish relatives. It was astonishingly like looking in the mirror. They were large, strong, robust, blonde and tall. She saw herself as a true Viking. She thought about how her entire family all had Viking cells cruising around in their bodies. She was proud that it was part of her heritage. The Vikings arrived in America long before Columbus. She realized that day why she had always been drawn to read about this native tribe of people.

Her parents had to learn to survive and raised themselves. Unconditional love, nurturing, safety and peace were never part of their experience when they were growing up. Consequently, her brother and sisters along with herself now understand why they were forced to grow up beyond their years. The emphasis was on work harder, take on lots of responsibility i.e. like cooking and cleaning. They were pushed to be over-achievers and were not allowed to complain. The O'Sullivan clan was raised not to show their feelings or even talk about them. Just do, without even a clue of how to just be.

Chapter 4

Age-Old Story of the Hatfield's and McCoy's Ours Was the O'Sullivan's and Loughty's

"Tension, in the long run, is a more dangerous force than any feud known to man."
~ Criss Jami, Killosophy~

I want to give you a brief overview of why you might not know the O'Sullivan side of the family. Why Ailill had never openly discussed her life, even with her children. Conversations about her and her family were never discussed because of the wedge of superiority and social status that loomed in their home like a brick wall. Her children were raised hearing their Dad saying things like, "Your Mom is who she is because of me. She was born on the wrong side of the tracks. I got her young so I could train her. She came from trailer trash. It took only a bottle of champagne and a steak to get her family to convince her to marry me;" Etc. Do you get the picture?

Remember, Ailill was into her victim mode, young, naive and had virtually no self-esteem at the time. She honestly believed that her children were raised to be ashamed of her which contributed to their inability to respect her or her heritage. Please know this is not about fault finding on anyone's part but it is the truth of what was an absolutely dysfunctional family. Looking back she wished she understood that being poor and hard-working was every bit as virtuous as wealth and social status. In her defense, she openly admitted in her diary that she was excited about the possibility of sharing this information with all of her loved ones in hopes that they could reconsider for themselves the disrespectful ugly stories they had heard about her.

She knew that some of the stories were based in fact but some had been taught due to being overly aggregated and simply not true. Every tribe of people has their stories and passes them on from generation to generation. My intention is just to add light and understanding, from her point of view. She graduated from high school in June of 1965 and married her first husband in November of that year. He was twenty-seven years old, still living at home and working for his family's company.

Ailill's parents aggressively pushed her into marrying him saying that she would never have an opportunity like this again and she felt coerced and had to do it. His parents, the rich Loughty's, came to her humble home and offered money to her parents to keep her from marrying their son. They likened her to a gold digger and validated the fact that their son was looking for a trophy wife. In fairness to her first husband, in his pursuit, wanting to marry her, he did move out of his parent's home a month before the wedding.

It wasn't until later in life that Ailill learned every one of us has the power of choice. In hindsight she realized that our choices are truly what shape our lives. Ailill honestly did not understand that at the time. She didn't think she had a choice. Her confusion came from an upbringing of listening for instructions and knowing you had to follow them. Her soon to be husband demanded she jump to his commands and her only question was how high.

Her sisters, Quinn and Reagan recently shared with her that to this day they did not understand her apprehension to marry him. They explained how they believed she lived the Cinderella story compared to their lives and future. The diversity in how we see each other is a real mystery and a marvel, is it not? As Ailill listened to their perspective, she could see the folly of her thinking. While I was reading Ailill's journal I was reminded how I love the twists and turns of life. If you don't like what is showing up in your life remember to hang on because it is guaranteed to change. This to shall pass is an accurate old cliché proven over and over again by all of us.

Speaking of twists and turns, Ailill's journey down memory lane was not a linear straight path. I realized it's more like a maze than a path. Back and forth, up and down, then around and around. Are you dizzy yet? I know I certainly was.

Before I introduce her brother and sisters I would like to highlight a few of her personal experiences growing up. Her brother and sisters are extremely close to Ailill and always have been throughout their entire lives. They are all now in our late 60s and

28

early 70s and when they shared their mutual memories they were amazed at how differently each one remembered the how, where and when of their personal stories.

One of her most acute and influential memories are when she was six years old. Ailill was admitted to the children's research hospital in Massachusetts. She was in terrible pain as a child and subsequently it was discovered that she was actually a twin that did not separate in the womb. Parts of her twin grew inside her body. In 1953 she was only the second person known to have had multiple organs, extra blood vessels and yet to be discovered body parts. She found it curious that she was born in June; this is the sign of twins and she was internally twins. Her memory was not sure how long she had to stay in the hospital but her childhood memory feels like it was a year. Maybe it was only three months, but it felt like a year. Her parents lived in New Hampshire so they were unable to come and visit her throughout her entire stay in the hospital. She underwent numerous exploratory surgeries and she was poked, prodded, and x-rayed. As she states in her journals;"It was without a doubt a walk through hell". Ailill remembered thinking she was abandoned and thrown away because she was a bad girl and that her parents just didn't want her anymore. She didn't understand that her brother and sisters were only two and four years old, and her mother was pregnant with her youngest sister.

She overheard her parents arguing and her mother crying because due to her medical bills they lost their little farm in New Hampshire. Ailill internalized the loss they had because of her at a very deep level. She believed that the stork had dropped her off at the wrong place because she was the worse thing that could have ever happened to a family. She wrote about how she wished she was dead. This was a theme for her which continued for many years culminating in two suicide attempts during her young life.

This experience had impacted her in a very negative way. Even at the end stages of her life she writes about her phobias concerning doctors and hospitals. When she had to take her own children to the emergency room for myriads of childhood mishaps, she would faint dead away as soon as she saw the medical staff.

Her medical records reportedly state that she is non-compliant and that she chooses to act against medical advice. Consequently, this deformity has contributed to many of her major health issues throughout her life. Brianna, Ailill's middle daughter has a humorous story concerning these issues. Brianna claims she has already had three wakes for her mother in this lifetime. She swears her mother has a life span of a cat with nine lives. Ailill wrote in her journal that when she does finally cry wolf for real, nobody will believe her. Ailill often wondered about this through the years, asking herself:" What does it mean"? She continues to knock on heavens door and they won't let her in.

Chapter 5

What Insanity Looks Like

"Don't worry if people think you're crazy. You are crazy. You have that kind of intoxicating insanity that lets other People Dream Outside of the lines and become who they're destined to Be."
~ Jennifer Elisabeth, Born Ready~

Remember when this grandmother described herself as passionate, wild, fanatical, mad, extremely foolish and unaware? I do not doubt that after reading this chapter you will agree with every adjective I used in describing Ailill.

During the years 1981 through 1992, Ailill made a trip down the rabbit hole. Like Alice in Wonderland, this part of her life was filled with mad hatters, crazy queens, potions, and spells. She wasn't able to identify or label the stressors at that time in her life. Life was disguised as humans who were as crazy as she was. She was struggling with early sobriety, not realizing that her emotional maturity was only that of a fourteen-year-old. She started as a teenager taking diet pills, uppers and downers, worked full time while going to school to just survive. Her venture down the rabbit hole lasted for another five years until she was able to accomplish her real long term sobriety in 1986. Ailill described how uncomfortable she felt in her body, she needed to undergo a series of extreme changes because her sense of self became disabled. It was during this time of her life that she discovered that without her chemical coper she didn't have any life skills. Her coper was broken. She had landed on a new planet where she didn't speak the language. She wrote that she didn't know how to dress and she felt like an alien to everything around her. She was uncertain of my own identity. Ailill butted heads with authority and strived to understand the seemingly arbitrary rules of the games that people played around her, even in death.

One of the things Ailill learned about sobriety was that she had to become willing to change her playgrounds and playmates. That was impossible because her playgrounds included her family, her husband, her children, cousins, aunts, uncles, and everything she knew and loved.

31

There is a funny story about the early months of her sobriety. Her parents, Mary & Maddox O'Sullivan, lived on twenty acres adjacent to hers in Idaho. Her two sisters, Quinn and Reagan, also lived in homes on the combined forty acres. Ailill came home from work one evening hearing the music in her sister's trailer and realized they were all having a party. They knew it was her but they pretended they weren't home. She knocked on the door crying and pleading with them to let her in. She promised them sobriety was not contagious. She later learned that her father had attended AA meetings. He swore the whole family to secrecy because he said, "That brainwashing cult seems to be working for Ailill. So don't tell her". Her sister, Reagan recently shared this with her. She had kept this secret for thirty years.

Her daughters, Brianna and Kaitlyn Loughty were living in an institution, her son had run away and Ailill was left alone in the dream that she had built for the four of them. Her children didn't want anything to do with her or living in a Podunk town in Idaho.

Changing Faces Youth Rehabilitation was a for-profit institution that was Mormon faith-based. The few family therapy sessions Ailill attended succeeded in convincing her and her two daughters that all of their life problems were because of her alcoholism and because she was their mother. It was all true; she knew her children would be better off with anyone but her. So she buried her head in the sand and took another exit. It was during this time that after losing everything Ailill took the sleeping pills and vodka. Talk about hitting a bottom, She learned that her best friend, being alcohol, no longer worked for her, it had become her worst enemy. From age fourteen to age forty Ailill lived in a foggy, unreliable, and unexplainable existence.

As I write this I am simply amazed when I think about the number of people Ailill could count as immediate family. The O'Sullivan Clan is 70 people strong. They have proven without a shadow of a doubt that they have inherited a genetic predisposition for alcoholism and addiction.

Ailill firmly believed there are absolutely no mistakes in God's world, that our destiny (has in some way) must have been charted long before we arrived. Each of us must be exactly where we are supposed to be. That would mean that each of us signed up for what she considered to be one of the most treacherous maladies known to man. Addiction is a challenge that encompasses paying a price physically, emotionally, spiritually and psychologically in life. It was incomprehensible, even for Ailill, to acknowledge how many of her family members are in early recovery, in recovery, struggling to get clean, in institutions, or just getting out of institutions, some having lived on the streets, gone to jail, and enduring broken relationships and have had to bury her loved ones due to their multi-generational genetic predisposition. This disease has not shown favoritism or sympathy because there was a very small number of the O'Sullivan clan that had escaped this particular taskmaster. The upside of this is that in her diary of a crazy alcoholic grandma it is a story about how she saw it. It took courage she didn't know she had to be able to share from her compassion and essence of her core. If Ailill didn't believe this was her last curtain call I don't think she would be able to stand before her family in her exposed brokenness of the past, nor shout her accolades of accomplishments. Remember in the beginning she wanted the letters to be delivered to her family only after she died.

In the last year before Kaitlyn, her youngest daughter's death, mother and daughter were able to share from their heart space all the brokenness. They openly talked about the years lost due to their shared addictions. Kaitlyn asked her if she understood why she just had to hate her mother for most of her life. She honestly shared with her daughter that she was very confused about that. Ailill told her daughter that is was her hope that thirty-three years of recovery, being the alcoholic, and becoming a drug counselor, helping hundreds of other people but not being able to reach her own daughter was extremely baffling. Ailill intended that living sober and clean, she dared to hope that she could be a living testament to amend the past. As an alcoholic addict, she experienced what the founders of AA called incomprehensible demoralization. This is another way of saying there is absolutely no way to describe the depths of her despair. Her youngest daughter said she had to hate her because just being in her presence made her feel like dog (chit). This is another example of why addiction is a disease of isolation. Kaitlyn also shared that she realized there was a loving God because He allowed her to pull the cancer card because she tried but never could acknowledge that she was an alcoholic. Can you begin to see how scary and challenging writing her memoirs was? She so desperately wanted to share her journey with all of her family in the hope they would find some understanding and gain some idea of who she was. I know I stand on solid ground when I say Ailill never talked about excuses. No blame was ever intended, only her truth and sharing. She was not writing to promote herself to some lofty position or to prove herself in her family's eyes. She only wanted to share a Little light that would possibly allow her loved ones to find forgiveness in their hearts so everyone could all come full circle in healing. The risk in sharing her journey was knowing full well that the outcome may mean that she might lose her family and that she would be abandoned. She wrote about her biggest fear being that they will stop all communication and she would be left to die alone and estranged from the ones she loved. There is another gift I discovered when reading Ailill's journals when she talked about how all of us truthfully are part of a soul family. She had sponsored and counseled hundreds of people who were the only alcoholic/addict in their family. Their challenges of being so misunderstood and alone, being the only black sheep in the family is something the O'Sullivan Clan never had to experience. They knew each other in a very intimate way due to traveling the same path hand in hand.

Ailill spoke about wanting to have an opportunity to share with everyone from a younger generation who has come under the demons of methamphetamine, opiates and more addictive drugs. This seasoned alcoholic great-grandmother realized she didn't even begin to understand the torture and strength of their demons and addictions. She knew that if she would have had the experiences they have, she admitted that she would have been dead a long time ago. She blessed them all, as they continued on their warrior's journey.

Her drafts of the parting letters to her grandchildren, great-grandchildren and adult children read like this: The clarity I have today, in God's Waiting Room, is the gift I want to give you. You will learn how to celebrate your life; however, it shows up for you. Sometimes you have to learn to let the wound heal in its own time. Every day can be a victory no matter where we are on our life path. There will be that day when you wake up and you'll know the fight is over. All the waiting has finally paid off and that you can breathe again. No More Pain in the chest and feeling like you're

34

running on a timeline. NO More wanting to stay in bed feeling like life has taken over.

It feels like VICTORY!! You want to go around dancing to your favorite song and stuffing your face with cake and ice cream again. DO IT! You earned it! You waited for the war to end, and fought the battle the right way. YOU DID IT! It was you who fought, you who conquered. Don't ever feel weak or fragile when you think you need help. Sometimes seeking help only gives you clarity. It takes courage to ask for help. It takes courage to face life.

There will be that day when you wake up and feel amazing because now you'll know what it's like to kick 'life' in the backside. You'll know what real victory feels like. Now you know suffering and beauty aren't separate. Follow your own life as close as possible. Follow the light, I promise it is so worth the journey. Learn to stop being who you thought you needed to be and discover your spirit. Opportunity is always masked as obstacles. We are all living our future, right now. I wrote this prayer in my journal, to release heaven to find it here on earth. Life is a terminal condition and we don't have to live for career, job, recognition, and material success. This great-grandmother is still a student of life. I would have you know that what I teach is so desperately what I need to learn. It is my truth that I am sharing with you but I have to remind myself repeatedly to drop from my head and stay in my heart. I have decided that fear just wastes air, COPD has been a great teacher.

Returning to her reminiscing, she knew she was blessed in those beginning years of being called upon to work at the Alcohol Recovery Center (ARC). Looking back she wondered if she could have ever stayed clean. Ailill surrounded herself with people in recovery. She opened her ranch up to recovering people. She had a large garden, raised a couple of cows, she still had eight horses, several peacocks, one pig, and two goats. She also had a colleague, Blade Dexter, who was her best friend and sidekick for many years who eventually became husband number three. They were both counselors at the ARC and their work together was almost magical. They were on the same wavelength. When they facilitated group therapy or marriage counseling everyone was amazed at how they could feed off each other in a way that left people thinking that they were reading minds or physic. Of the thirteen years during their friendship, they were married for only five of those.

In early recovery Ailill admitted she still had a bad boy magnet. She repeatedly attracted men who were confused, broken, angry, lost and narcissistic. Why not, it felt like a match. Blade's charisma was beyond measure, he was on fire with the love of God as he understood Him. His passion was to play in praise bands; he was an incredibly talented drummer. It was a very tumultuous thirteen years. He would continually relapse, but Ailill kept hanging on. You know the feeling when it is good, it is so good, almost euphoric, and when it is bad it can lead you right down that rabbit hole. It's the crisis and chaos, of peaks and valley's, which kept her hooked on her adrenaline.

Ailill was led to believe that their destiny was forever linked even when she would run away. She relapsed with Blade at five years sober. The consequence of his relapse was severe. The judge made an example of him because he knew Blade was an alcohol and drug counselor. He was sentenced to six months in jail after having several years of sobriety. It was while he was in jail that Ailill put the log cabin and horse ranch up for sale, loaded up the U- haul and headed for California.

Ailill's relapse was equally eventful. She was in a drunken blackout even before she experienced getting a buzz on. She didn't remember calling her boss who was the director of the Malheur County Mental Health Department while she was drunk. She went back to work the following Monday morning pretending, or so she thought, that it was just a regular workday. The staff had already worked up a probationary period of 90 days with things she had to accomplish because they decided that they needed her to stay in the position she was holding. Can you imagine the humiliation and embarrassment? One more time Ailill so wanted to be somebody she wasn't. As luck would have it, this happened on a day she was in charge of a women's group therapy session. The women proceeded in pulling off her covers because they knew she had relapsed that weekend. They confronted her with her own psychobabble. They said, "You have preached to us from the beginning that no matter what, don't pick up the habit again and all will be well". She knew at that moment they were right. She quit her job that day as a counselor.

When she arrived in California she lived with her son and daughter- in- law, Dean and Mary Doughty who were now into their own recovery. Ailill struggled with trying to put some clean time together. After fully committing herself and working hard she knew she had to get back to the very beginning and start over with being rigorously honest with herself. She was able to complete the required clean time and went to work for the Salvation Army Rehabilitation Center in San Diego California. Dr. Latté became not only her boss but also a mentor and spiritual advisor. He was an Irish Priest who left the priesthood to become the director of the treatment center. He concentrated on helping her through Adult Children of Alcoholics and Alanon. Dr. Latte' complimented her leaving Idaho and finally breaking away from being in love with a man who suffered from chronic relapse. She came to realize how blatant her codependent issues were. Ailill wanted to fix the world by investing herself so totally that she had no boundaries. Looking back she had to laugh at herself, but it was OK that she worked 80 hours, 7 days a week and had a caseload of 80 people. She was so Co- dependent that she got paid for it for 40 years total. As I share her story, I realize anyone can attest to being co-dependent. It has become a popular, over used and abused word. All of us, who love too much, repeatedly forsake all personal limitations. The outcome is always lots of twists, turns, and heartbreaks.

She was at work one day when a probation officer asked her if I knew the praise band drummer from the rescue center who was from Hood River Oregon. How many praise band drummers can there be from Hood River Oregon? When she walked into the center and saw Blade, not knowing they were on the same block, he ran down the stairs and she didn't see him again. Until one day she heard over the intercom that she had a visitor waiting for her in the lobby. She was just finishing up a therapy session before she went to see who it was. The receptionist directed her to Dr. Latte's office. Dr. Latte was fully aware of who Blade was. Remember, when she mentioned his charismatic personality. He wasn't even looking for a job but he was hired, right on the sport, to work right alongside her. You can see why Ailill decided it was a destiny call, an omen telling her no matter what, she was not going to get away. Coincidence is God saying Hi, or so she thought. This had to mean he was her true soul partner. Because now they both worked for the Salvation Army a Christian based institution. We had to get married. Even though she loved him deeply, she cried all night long knowing deep inside herself that she was in for a very rocky road. She was living alone on her 36' foot sailboat, she was happy as a clam, and she was aware that storms were brewing on her horizons.

Long story short, Blade continued to relapse. He burglarized their office stealing computers, furniture, etc. and leaving Ailill without a car as they shared only one because he now lived on the sailboat and worked at the same place. He stole the sailboat one day to sail to Mexico, now leaving her without a home. Ailill called the Coast Guard. She learned that in his drunken, drugged-out state he yelled at them while they hovered over him in a helicopter. He wanted to know when it was that the Coast Guard got involved with marital disputes.

The last straw was when Blade took a busload of clients to LA and stopped at the liquor store and ended up in intensive care. He did suffer from acute PTSD as he was a specialized medic in Vietnam. Dr. Latte fired Ailill because his driver's license had been revoked for five years. Dr. Latte held her responsible for not letting him know about Blade's suspended license. She had worked there before Blade came back into her life but she was once again living in the wake of destruction and disaster in her own recovery.

Blade and Ailill went to work from there to Denver Colorado at the Outdoors Wilderness Resort. It was on 120 acres with rock climbing, river rafting and activities for City Kids who had lost their way. The Outdoors resort also served corporations which allowed them to finance working with juveniles. Ailill used all her savings, sale of her ranch and retirement funds to build a restaurant and home as they were told they were founding partners. One more time being excessive compulsive, goal-oriented and workaholics they developed this wonderful business. Blade relapsed again disappearing for a week, she thought he was dead. Being a faith-based company her partners persuaded her to give Blade another chance. The next relapse was when she walked into their living room and he was celebrating his fifty-second birthday with some old Vietnam buddies. Ailill packed up the car and headed to Oregon where her sober friends lived. The last time she saw him, he looked at her with his giant pale blue eyes and begged her not to be mad, he said," That he would get back on the wagon tomorrow".

Blade died of an accidental overdose two hours later. It took the coroner's office three days to find Ailill in Oregon. His death certificate read accidental overdose. She wondered, "Was it suicide? Did he do it to spite me"? Ailill's grief for the next five years was unbearable. They sold Outdoors Wilderness Resort and because she received a paycheck the board of directors considered her an employee and not a partner. In one day, she was fifty-two years old; Ailill lost her husband, her home, restaurant, chuck wagon, and a lifetime of savings. She had expected so much more from a Christian based organization she couldn't believe this was happening to her. Her adult children abandoned her at this point. Her burdens were just too much for them. She couldn't blame them they now had their own families.

She buried Blade on a Friday and went to work the following Monday. This private out-patient association had five locations throughout Oregon. She couldn't afford to move her furniture, bury her husband and make the first and last payment on an apartment. A woman who owned a small studio in her backyard gave her a roll-away-bed and a card table. She was all alone and didn't know a soul when she was transferred to Hood River Oregon. Ailill remembered writing in her journal that night talking to God complaining, feeling sorry herself and blaming fate for her terrible plight. She asked God, "What's going on here, do you want me to live as a monk?" The wrong question, the next morning she totaled her Bronco on black ice on my way to Carson to teach a DUI class. Ailill was now on a bicycle her sister, Quinn gave her for the next six months. Lesson learned, she would never shake my fist at God again and decided pity parties would never get her anywhere and be careful what you pray for because if you say it out loud the power of attraction will possibly manifest it for you. What we all must remember the universe is always listening.

That next month Ailill was enmeshed in deep grief when a book fell off the shelf while she was in the director's office. Her boss said he knew it was meant for her as it almost literally hit her on the head. The title of the book was Conversations with God, by Donald Neal Walsch. She knew if God could speak to her directly

39

today this would be exactly what she needed to learn from her life's journey thus far.

Ailill's heart was broken so wide open that she now knew that her inner consciousness was becoming the experience of a new person. Intuitively she knew she had to accomplish these life lessons for her souls' growth because she intuitively knew she came here determined to get a Ph.D. in soul growth. From that moment on, she planned not to miss a thing and she hasn't. Ailill believed this is Earth school and in the big eternal picture, she likened it to a two-week bad camping trip.

When you change everything changes. This is an overview of the article Ailill wrote for the Vision Newspaper. She wrote about what change looks like:

"Change the way you look at things and the things you look at change." "Change is painful, but nothing is as painful as staying stuck somewhere you don't belong." "Those who cannot change their minds cannot change anything." "All things are difficult before they are easy."

Some of the most life-changing quotes of change can generally affect our lives.

- Kindness changes everything. ...
- Maybe it's not about fixing something but starting over again. ...
- Never quit, if you stumble get back up. ...
- It's time to start something new and trust the magic of beginnings.
- This is where I start my comeback.

Chapter 6

Inner Knowing

Ailill's morning prayers and meditation was her usual practice for over fifty years. Her years of journaling have created volumes of inspirations, AaHa moments, articles and memories. She would usually mentally rehearse her gratitude list daily. This had become such an easy spiritual discipline because she became hooked on her intuitive moments. She knew that these are the moments when you know that something greater than you is communicating with you. She likened it to a tuning fork that was broadcasting the messages from the Sacred. She had learned not to push against it and not to question it. The unexpected knowing usually speaks to something she was unaware of. It took her to a place of recognizing that it is always an answer or enlightening message to what she had been thinking about, worried about or had been curious about. In other words; enlightenment happens when you least expect it. She often wrote about the Universal Life Force that has an amazing sense of humor. When she did push against it, she got this niggling sense of a smile saying; "Bargaining again with God Ailill, has that ever worked for you?"

She had this wonderful little story that she shared over the years, particularly with her adolescent clients whose imagination and visualization skills are at an all-time high point in their life.

There was once upon a time two little fish that lived in the sea. One day they began discussing God. They discussed amongst themselves that they had never seen God or heard God, so where is God they wondered? They decided to embark on a journey to find God. They swam the Pacific Ocean, the Atlantic Ocean, and the Red Sea. Beginning to get weary and frustrated from their long search they saw this huge grandfather fish. He is wise and old they thought, he'll know where to find God, Let's ask him. When they explained to Grandfather Fish how far they had traveled and what they were looking for, he voluntarily explained, "Boys, God is in the water." They remained confused as he swam away. She loved this story because she believed God is so obvious we miss Him. The source of God is the air between us, our next breath, love, the stars and plants. What we are looking for, we are looking with, and the joke is on us. Ailill had placed her idea of God so far away before she discovered that the Holy Spirit resides in all things; she realized God is omnipresent, omnipotent, and omniscient as is the energy of all things created. She loved physics because for her it is proof of what she believed. She learned that everything in the universe is made of the same neutrons, protons and structure and we are all made of the same stuff. The only difference between animate and inanimate objects is the rate of speed at which these particles vibrate. The slower the speed the more solid material objects appear. Back when, in her classes and group therapies, everyone would laugh at her when she shared how excited she was when the rock that Neil Armstrong brought back from the moon in 1969 was proven to be made of the same old stuff.

In God's waiting room one morning she had one of those Aa-Ha moments and realized how she continued to join in that ocean of the unknown. She came back to California after her husband died and her son, Dean found her an apartment in an Active Senior Citizen community in Santa Maria. Ailill was fifty-five years old, still working, had a car and she was once again doing life. To her amazement, 90% of the residents were actively participating in their own God's waiting room. Most had given up and were on hold. They would line up at her door needing bread, sugar and their prescriptions filled, etc. She became so overwhelmed that she resorted to coming home after dark, not turning on her lights and sneaking in so no one saw her. In her diary while laying in bed those thirteen months she suddenly realized that was 17 years ago. Laughingly, she remembered thinking she was old then and living her last chapter at that time. She had no idea that she would go forward to opening two new businesses, launch a career as an artist, become a Reiki Master, teach at a college, learn about Aura's and Chakra's and do insightful energy readings for over 2000 people. She had adamantly resolved to never get married again as she believed her destiny spelled disaster in that area of her life. In re-reading her journals she realized she had an existence that no one could ever possibly have imagined. Highlighted, by traveling the world, kayaking, and riding zip lines, camping trips and hundreds of hours snorkeling. Her husband and Ailill may need to seek therapy. Yes, she did remarry after all but therapy is mentioned here jokingly because in all the years they have been married they have not had a single fight. They do compromise most lovingly. She wondered if when she was eighty-nine years old if she will playfully be able to see the downtime she was experiencing now as just another bump in the road. Whenever her friends or I pass that senior community it has become customary to give thumbs up and say out loud, "You've come a long way Baby." We just can't know what's around the next corner and what God has in store for us. Every single being has an unfathomable gift, meeting life head-on gives us the ability to be as alive as possible. The purpose of the human experience is for the soul to blossom right here on earth. Exploration and learning have been a wonderful part of her life, but in the end, she realized all of us have to surrender to exactly what it is. Ailill had read thousands of books over the years, taken lots of classes, attended seminars and gleaned inspiration and knowledge from hundreds of mentors who will never know how powerfully they impacted her life. She had not read a novel just for pleasure in sixty years because her curiosity, thirst for knowledge and awe of spirituality, soul, spirit, and love for God was unquenchable. Each of us is a novel and each of us is the hero or heroine of our own story. Ailill loved people so much that she wrote that she wished she could meet all of the seven billion humans on this planet and still fervently want to know more about each one. Ailill knew we are not small; each one of us is a unique creation so stunningly spectacular and complex that we sometimes don't realize that we alone are the ones we've been looking for. She shared with everyone that: You and I are God's idea. It just doesn't get any better than that. We can not bypass the human experience because you and I are already God's best idea, even though we don't always realize it. You are your best self right now. Ailill learned that if she never flirted with failure she would never have been able to dance with joy. Everything in creation contains a special purpose.

Life is shaped from the inside out. If we never went within through prayer, meditation, wonder and truly listening to our intuition, we will have gone without. If we don't go within you will go without.

Meditation is simple. It is just taking time to be quiet within yourself', whether it's five minutes or a half-hour.

Ailill talked to God all day. Meditation for her was when she got quiet and actively set a time to listen to God. Meditation can happen for all of us, maybe when we're working in the garden or painting a picture or even preparing a meal. Meditation is when we enter a zone and just be present with what is. Time at that moment is blank and there's an underlying peace and bliss that is always there. All we have to do is become aware of it. Ailill believed in and lived by that old age cliché, "Keep it simple stupid". Ailill spent years learning how to meditate, she found out there is only one way. That one way is our way. She would encourage everyone to find their own way. Take what fits and throw the rest away.

Ailill loved to share one of the most powerful utterances of her soul; it's a quick message to redefine success, which means more to her today than ever before. She realized she was the most successful when she knew how to give up what no longer works for her. Whenever she sought to live by what she thought others expectations of her were, she came to know that she just took a left turn and walked towards fear. It was always the beginning of another lesson she just didn't want to learn. To help overcome her chronic people-pleasing personality she had to change her thinking. She came to believe and know that the Universal Source of all positively works in her favor. It was never about her analyzing the beat of the drummer that others listened to. Life can always be a positive experience for us if we don't judge by appearances and trust that the Universal Source of all shows up in unimaginable disguises. When Ailill could stay in the space of being very practical, knowing that this too shall pass, she was able to help herself from becoming so totally invested in the outcome. Nelson Mandela says it so beautifully, "Live life as though nobody is watching, and express yourself as though everyone is listening." I recently heard someone say it doesn't matter if the glass is half full or half empty as long as you have a pitcher standing by.

Ailill used to rush here and there, always in a hurry until the universe put the brakes on. How in the world was she going to be able to cultivate happiness when she got most of her kudos in life from doing? Defining success, she wrote doesn't have to look like anything and it doesn't have to be anything particular. It doesn't mean pleasure. She depressingly thought she was going to miss the joyfulness in the experience of striving for her potential. What was she going to do now? Ailill's unhappiness invited her into a deep inner introspection. If happiness was being optimistic, how could she now be optimistic lying in bed for 12 months? Her journal writings began to reflect the idea that she could redefine success for herself. She had proven to herself by reading auras through bio-

44

feedback that gratitude changes our frequency. She knew she had to write it down, use visualization to experience a physic change or depression would continue to overtake her. So she developed an exercise of imagining that she was sending Thank You notes to everyone and everything as an attempt to work through these dark times. Ailill had to create methods she had not used before because she was unable to do anything she did before. Her fragile place was fraught with medical professionals saying she was a mystery and beyond their expertise. She couldn't talk about it out loud or that would make it real. Ailill asked herself, "How was I going to transform this infirmed reality?"

Ailill taught for years that by renewing your mind you can change your world. In this particular trial when she would read her journals back to herself she had the experience of feeling like a fraud, liar, and hypocrite. She had reached a place where her invisible tool belt which contained life-giving messages didn't work anymore. What she did know was that she had to feed her happiness or it would continue to die. She had always agreed with Abraham Lincoln, "You are as happy as you make up your mind to be." He suffered from chronic depression and found a way to transcend his genetic makeup. Everyone is in search of the same thing which is happiness. What does happiness look like?

Ailill found it again when she was forced to accept her powerlessness. Her husband, John through this trial, had been nothing short of an earth angel in real life. This last year he has had to do all the cooking, cleaning, taking her to doctors and held her hand during her meltdown periods of being in pain, being so sick and feeling like a beached whale. She came to realize, as he did, that she was not wired to be dependent on anyone. Her feelings of being a burden were crippling her. Her husband learned to cook gourmet meals. He built planter boxes and planted a garden so she could watch her garden grow. Ailill was the gardener in the family because he said he had a black thumb. She had always loved to cook but she now got the privilege of watching him as he developed a new exciting passion. He claims it wasn't that big of a deal because he had watched her for fourteen years. Ailill told him that she could only hope that if the shoe was on the other foot she would be half the caregiver he is. He has never once complained or suggested she was a burden, quite the opposite. He showed her what an honor and pleasure he felt in doing everything for her. Her family and friends praised his angelic dedication and he responded by just turning red and denying the compliments. Many had offered to come and stay so he could have a break, he declined saying he doesn't want to miss a minute with her. Through him, she came to know Grace which is the recognition of truly being loved unconditionally.

Ailill couldn't go and do anything. Grace is a gift. She got an up-close and personal experience of receiving Grace because she had nothing left to give. Life has meaning at every stage. She slowly found a new pair of glasses and watched as they shared games, meals, and movies. She had free time to read and pray. She recognized where she was blocking the gifts of Grace. This is when she wrote in her journal:"If this experience lasts forever what quality is it that I need for peace of mind?" Ailill would go out into her private beautiful healing room and do Reiki on herself. John had created the exact image she had of what it should look like when he had built this room for her. It was for the first time that she ever really pampered herself by taking time and soaking in the benefits of her work for others. Learning how to receive it for herself she discovered anew the real beauty in all the paintings she had created over the years. She was opening up to surprises and transformation. She practiced living in a new vibration and challenged her damaged view of herself. She learned that pain pushes you, until she was pulled into a larger vision with new potentials. Ailill slowly began to move away from the sensation of living in the dark night of the soul and pushing back even though her back was up against the wall. She spent months of pushing away family and friends because she didn't know how to share her darkness and weakness. When her home nurses, doctors, medical staff, family or friends did push their way in she suited up and showed up with a happy face and spouted joy and pretended to be strong. She was so ill that her husband was the only one aware that her insides didn't match her outsides. Everyone knew how sick she was as the hospice nurse counseled her husband on how to not resuscitate even with CPR because surviving a stroke would only further complicate her quality of life. The diagnosis was always about the final call. Ailill had spent a lifetime of being social. Aloneness was a brand new wrinkle.

Before going to the hospital thirteen months ago Ailill wasn't on any medications except for emergency inhalers, mild sleeping pills, and aspirin when needed. She was working with holistic healing practices. At last count, she had fifteen different prescriptions, four for high blood pressure, insulin, heart pills, etc. She felt poisoned this last year, with weakness, dizziness, shakes, painful diarrhea for hours and tremendous stomach pain from medications. What is different today is that against medical advice and her husband's fears, she stopped taking them all a few weeks ago. She knew she may have to revisit insulin but now she was up and I am writing her memoirs. She has all the same serious medical issues but she doesn't feel poisoned. Her family has asked her if she had a death wish. The answer is a resounding NO. She will admit she was hoping for relief this last year but here I am sharing my diary to whoever will read these words. Ailill had a new joy and a new project. She didn't consider herself a quitter; she gave it a year of pharmaceuticals in hopes of healing. She went to a meeting the other night and she was chastised for driving herself as she was still obviously far from 100%, but they hadn't seen her before. She feels blessed that she has refused taking any mood-altering pain pills. Doctors have tried to prescribe them at different times explaining that it would make her feel better and that she would like them. She had to explain to them, "That's the problem!" She would like them too much". She was still terrified about activating the phenomenon of craving. One will be too many and 1000, not enough, because once an addict always an addict.

Reading Ailill's journal I found a story where she wrote one line sentences. It seemed obvious to me that she was trying to resolve within herself what she could and could not control. The perplexity and puzzlement of her life led her to look for resolution in accepting the fragments of her experiences.

Grow Where You're Planted and Want What You Have

"We didn't choose to be Irish, German, Indian or Asian.
The design for a living started in the womb.
The patterns of destiny were born to bloom.
The cosmic conception had a divine ideal.
Where each of us will grow and where it will be.
To want what we have is not of this world.
The media pushes and pushes for more and more.
They spend billions to let us know that glamour is the goal.
Body size, and youth are better than soul.
The brainwashing worked for glamour, extravagance, and
opulence is everywhere.
Now our power still isn't enough.
Now we need pills to alter our reality and numb out.
Only to experience and discover how real is spiritual bankruptcy.
Take off the blinders and you will see that exterior of instant fixes.
More education and riches is now our God.
Is just a ploy to get us to wish and wish and crave more and more.
Wanting what you have you see, could threaten consumer
consumption.
Wanting what we have would mean lesser sales,
Advertising appeals to greed and luxury.
We now run harder, go faster, do more?
Only to learn we want more and more.
Now we have lost the eyes that see.
The allure of possessions is now center stage.
Going beyond balance has dulled our senses,
They got us to compete and compare.
It appealed to our vanity, greed, and need for power,
Our attitudes of gratitude are losing charm.
We buy the lie of needing more.
Greener pastures is our aim,
The happiness we think is when I'm rich or get that diploma.
Get married or buy that dream house.
Oh how did we forget, love, shelter, and harmony.
It is still beautiful and warm in every neighborhood.
That short or tall, slender or large, rich or poor are only labels.
Not the truth of the growing soul.
Riches and fame is an empty game.

The people we love and who loves us is far beyond rich or deprived,
The advertising magic has cast its spell, we are in danger.
Real peril of changing our wants to needs,
The technology has mesmerized us to depart from the soul.
Guidance of spirit is considered trivial and old.
Forgetting to nourish our spiritual needs is why we feel empty.
We need to fill the hole in our souls,
Happiness is not superior and most.
Happiness wants only what you have.
We have so much, how could we ever believe we need more and more.
When we can't begin to want what we already have.
This journey so short and we pretend we can take a U-haul behind the Hearst.
The riches and knowledge only tempers us for now.
We have forgotten the soul growth.
We once wanted dignity, character and grace.
Now instant gratification is substituted for contentment.
How fleeting and empty will the miles be without love, passion, joy?
Forgotten celebrations and the love of self need to become popular
Eternity is where we came from and where we will go back to.
Have we forgotten what will be the real lasting treasures of our short human journey? Count your blessings every day and watch how they grow and grow.
The moments of experience in the now are the Hidden treasures.
It is the soul place where we will grow and grow.

Begin to know we have always only wanted what we already have.
The design of destiny told me so.

49

Chapter 7

The Meaningful Unsung Heroes

"It was only after her death that I realized who she was:
The apparently magical force at the center of our family who'd
kept us all invisibly spinning in the powerful orbit around her."
~Cheryl Strayed, Wild: From Lost to Found on the Pacific Crest
Trail~

Ailill has always felt that coincidence is God saying "Hi."
Coincidence is when the timing of events is so unexpected,
surprising and so personally recognizable that we just know that
they were divinely orchestrated just for us. She would often reflect
on how many hundreds of pieces had to come together and become
obvious at the perfect right time. Coincidence for Ailill was the
proof of God's hand leading everyone and she learned that our
universe does always have our back in spite of appearances.

One morning she wrote about her recognition of just such a
moment. She wrote about the perfect timing of the universe just
before she received a call from her sister-in-law, Teagan
O'Sullivan. Tearfully, Teagan shared that Ailill's' younger brother
had only hours left to live according to his Hospice nurse.

Maddox O'Sullivan Jr. passed away November 4, 2019, at 9:50
p.m. at the age of 70. This last year Ailill and her brother shared
almost daily the experiences they were having while being in
God's waiting room. They faced timed almost daily the last week
of his life. Maddox was alert, cracking jokes, and telling her over
and over again how much he loved her. They often talked at four in
the morning when everyone else was still asleep. They discussed
openly and honestly what it was like to know they were close to
death. Both agreed they didn't fear dying, they just feared the
process. Ailill wrote in her journal that she wished everyone could
have been a fly on the wall as they laughed, shared from the heart,
and reviewed all of their life experiences. Some of their playful
attitudes may have been considered morbid as they shared their joy
of living as long as they had. In fact, it was an exciting miracle and
they shared their true unbelievable sense of being victorious.

The O'Sullivan clan is not known for longevity. Their father, Maddox O'Sullivan died at age 56 and their mother, Mary O'Sullivan age 61. Their aunts and uncles all died in their 40's. They realized that their mother passed away twenty-nine years ago and their father died thirty-four years ago. Ailill and Maddox grew up knowing they would die young. Reagan their middle sister remembered that retirement and getting old was never talked about. They never had any role models that prepared them for the expedition of living in an aging body. Never did they hear the words retirement as it was a multi-generational improbability. It was an excepted fact that they would die young and be good looking corpses.

Ailill and Maddox had been inseparable throughout their lives. Their bond was beyond description. The hole that it left in Ailill's life broke her heart wide open. She knew that whatever or wherever she was he would always be there for her. He could be a sassy kid. Sometimes he was considered a bully but his one true characteristic was his generosity. Maddox would take his hard earned allowance and buy candy and gifts for his three sisters. He truly would give anyone his last shirt on his back. He carried this legacy on in his fifty years of marriage and with his two sons and four granddaughters and two great-grandchildren. He joined the Marines at the age of seventeen and served twenty-eight years, he was known as Gunny Sergeant Maddox O'Sullivan. His son posted this message last week:

Maddox O'Sullivan Jr.
Synopsis:
The president of the United States takes pleasure in presenting the Silver Star medal to Maddox O'Sullivan, Lance Corporal, U.S. Marine Corps, for conspicuous gallantry and intrepidity in action while serving with Marine Attack Squadron 211 (VMA-211), 1st Marine Aircraft Wing, in connection with combat operations against the enemy in the Republic of Vietnam on March 21st, 1969. By his courage, aggressive fighting spirit and steadfast devotion to duty in the face of extreme personal danger, Lance corporal O'Sullivan upheld the highest tradition of the Marine Corps, and the United States Naval Service
Hometown, Boise, Idaho

Ailill wrote in her journal that she was apprehensive about sharing her thoughts while she was in this dark space of grief again. The grief process for her was not discriminating but all-encompassing of the darkest night of the soul. It triggered all the loses of her life, as if one more time she had taken the lid off Pandora's Box and the shadowy murky power that accumulates over time was devastatingly overwhelming. The death of parents when she was young, her husband of only five years who after thirteen years of shared recovery and working together in recovery, died at age 52 of an accidental overdose. Her youngest daughter dying of cancer at age 42, after fighting for her life for thirty six months, leaving her grandchildren ages six and seven without a mother. Her stepdaughter, Ann Barley only three months after her daughter's death, was diagnosed with fourth stage cancer and died at age 44. Her step-daughter also bravely fought for twenty seven months. Ailill and her husband spent seven and half years doing everything they could to be next to their daughters as they fought for their lives. Ailill's best friend of forty-five years and her maid of honor died three years ago and now her little brother left only two days ago.

Ailill wrote about feeling wretched in emotional pain that day. Her numerous losses cried out as she wrote:" It's against the regulations of righteousness, and the pattern of the universe to be such a young adult orphan. No one is supposed to be a widow at age fifty-two. You aren't intended to bury your children. I am the oldest of my siblings and I was supposed to go home first".

All of these precious souls were the meaningful unknown and unsung hero's and celebrities of her life. She realized she could write an entire book, about the impact of all the challenges, love, lessons and gifts each one had given her on her life's' journey.

How fast life can change. One week before her brother died she wrote about the powerful love connection she and her brother shared. At that particular moment, in the space of giving, receiving blessings and thanking God for the most wondrous gift of unconditional love her brother had always given her. Ailill was moved to write words of intention because she believed so strongly in the power of the word. He showed her that day when he was close to his transition that the best, very best time of life is when we are presenting as our unique self.

She was able to openly absorb his essence and see a magnificent one of a kind soul who will never be repeated thousands of years backward or forward no matter what our spiritual or religious beliefs are. She saw in a big way the light shine in his soul and knew it was the center of his eternal spirit. This moment of reinforcement reminded her what is available in every human being: Love, Compassion, Kindness, and Service. Our creator never makes a mistake and we are all on the journey of soul growth in its unfolding. In the end, Love is all there is!

Being in the process of grief she wrote: "No wonder I am certifiably crazy". She described it as having what she understood as a true bi-polar feeling. The battle between the light and dark can be so confusing. "Will the real me please stand up....wonder who that is"? In her grief she recognized it was when she asked the disempowering questions; "Why me? What's wrong?" One phrase she, herself had repeated over and over again in her counseling and teaching career was; "Grow where you are planted and Want what you have".

She understood she was a child of the universe because she was having a two-year-old tantrum. She angrily rebelled by writing, "I don't want what I have. People I dearly love are leaving me behind. My alignment with my truest higher self just doesn't show up until I give up my resistance. Until I can heal and forgive myself enough to surrender I will continue to block my blessings. I must have signed up for the school of hard knocks because (one more time) I am broken wide open when I don't practice letting life show up on life's terms and allow that to be OK."

Ailill continued to vent all her mixed emotions in her journal. She was amazed at this juncture how unstable her reality had become. She found that she was experiencing total stark raving fear associated with bats in her stomach and feeling nauseous. Her silent prayer throughout was wondering if her soul was capable of allowing the truth to be fully realized, which was that she could find the courage and the strength within herself to endure being so emotionally vulnerable.

Her attempts to release the lie of her unworthiness continued to rear its ugly head. She desperately wanted to overcome being anxious about whom and what she was. She was confronted again desperately struggling against her learned survival skills and her lifelong challenge of always sugar coating the truth. Denial wanted an audience. By choosing to see only rainbows one could deny the storm. Pretending to be stronger than she was, she needed to get over the fear of thinking about what everybody else might think, say or feel as she allowed me to expose her truest, deepest private fears and feelings.

Her entire family had become experts at taking names, keeping score, and kicking butt. They would then communicate in a triangle of victim, persecutor, and rescuer. She knew these strategies as well as she knew she was a main contributor. She knew why this was a momentous, earth-shattering, consequential, and eventful task. It was the idea of being rigorously honest with herself and sharing that with everyone which was so important to her due to her ticking time clock. Ailill expressed to me the urgency in wanting to get honest with her family. It was now or never. She knew she needed, for once in her life to get real about the ongoing estrangements within her family.

Estrangements with family are one of the most psychologically painful experiences anyone could experience. This ostracizing of family members from family is counter-intuitive. Who, after all, would think to terminate a relationship with the ones closest to you like your own daughter's, son, or the parents who raised you? Ailill didn't want to be estranged from anyone. Sadly, the answer is that it's typically only people who feel they have been neglected, abused, or exploited in some way who would pursue such a tumultuous split. When anyone triggered her pain buttons she couldn't fight the inclination of resorting to her old behaviors. When the choice between fight and flight presented itself she would run and hide where you couldn't find her. Some say, "Fear is; false illusions appearing real". For Ailill, when faced with conflict, it was, "F@&% everything and run."

She didn't want to use the word regret because she had learned that each of us is entitled to the life we lived and are living. It is from this hard-won wisdom that she now had the gift of re-seeing from the vantage point of finally claiming what has been. She could now see beyond the trials and tribulations to their inherent meaning.

A long life taught Ailill that if we see each other as small in any way we are denying our own identity. If we don't see the Christ divinity in each other, we are supporting a lie. All of us, are not who we are in our human small self. Ailill expressed joy as she felt blessed to have come to an understanding that she couldn't participate in the folly anymore. She was also blessed to have the opportunity finally to acknowledge and express the divine beauty that she saw that resides in each and everyone she had ever loved, and even in those that she thought she did not love. To know truth is to know that your soul will agree because our soul knows we are all one. Every one of us are not the mistakes we've made because that's not who we are, only what we did in ignorance and fear.

Ailill honestly admitted to herself that there was no excuse or justification for how she pursued such behaviors which caused the tumultuous split with her own three children. Her youngest daughter's death is the event that brought all these painful experiences to the forefront of her life to be examined and relived.

Ailill's children were only 11, 12 and 13 years old when she and their dad got a divorce. In their 16 and half years of marriage, they had become very successful according to the world's measurement of material wealth. They lived in a 6000 square foot Tutor mansion with a Rolls Royce and Lamborghini parked in their driveway. They started from practically nothing, living in a very small apartment to creating a large restaurant chain throughout California.

Upon reflection, she could see that her children suffered terribly from abandonment and neglect as she and her husband lived, breathed and talked only about their work and personal ambitions. Looking back she saw how superficial, plastic and unreal their lifestyle had become. It was all about keeping up with the Joneses, entertaining so-called friends from the country club and yacht club. Ailill said so-called friends because they all disappeared when the prestige and money ran out.

The aftermath of the divorce continued to be bitter and hateful. It was at this time Ailill decided she had to extract the silver spoon from her children's mouths and somehow, someway teach them honesty, real values, integrity, and reliability. That was her goal; she just didn't know how she was going to get there.

Today, Ailill and her three children laugh at the memory of how she packed up the U- haul truck, her 3 kids and off they went. They flipped a coin at each intersection to see which way they were going to go and where they would land to start their new life. They ended up in Hood River Idaho (the population was 500 including cats and dogs) where she bought 20 acres next to her parent's 20-acre horse ranch. Her parents gave her ten horses in payment for a loan from years ago. Ailill had absolutely no idea about how to run an Arabian horse ranch but she no longer had a dream of her own so embracing her parents dream with absolutely no knowledge of what she was in for seemed like a fair substitute at the time. She laughed at herself as she fantasized about her grandchildren learning about their parent's experience of being uprooted in their adolescence.

Her very best intentions turned out to be one of the worst nightmares she could have ever imagined. All three teenagers were so distraught that they accused her of moving them to the end of the world compared to where they came from. She tried to make light of the situation by telling them this is not the end of the world, you just feel like you can see it from here. The culture shock was unimaginably challenging. They couldn't believe that people carried guns in the windows of their pickups. Her youngest daughter, Kaitlyn, ran up the stairs crying wearing her beautiful gown and gloves when her date for the prom showed up in Levis and a tee shirt. It was no laughing matter when the local farmers referred to her children as the punk rockers from California. Ailill's girlfriend from Hood River Idaho says they are still talking about them. This is when everything started on the destruction, separation, and annihilation downslide. She had a full-fledge teenage mutiny on her hands and the only disciplinary, respected parent was no longer in the picture.

By the time her children were fourteen, fifteen and sixteen they were placed in intuitions and ran away. They never returned to her home to live as a family again. The tragic predicament of her actions and choices began the cycle of hate, rejection, isolation, and abandonment from her children. Her two daughters, Brianna and Kaitlyn actively spewed their hatred towards her for the next twenty-four years.

Ailill compounded their distrust by a suicide attempt in 1983. She knew she had failed as a wife; mother, daughter and now learned that she couldn't even drink or enjoy drugs like normal people. That's when she went in the middle of the hayfield and popped a bottle of sleeping pills and chased them down with vodka. She woke up in the hospital with paddles on her chest. She had been pronounced dead for several minutes. Her daughter, Brianna came to the hospital and said:" You are the only parent I have. I can't believe you don't love me enough to want to live." There are no words to describe the depth of Ailill's shame.

The life after death experience Ailill had was so powerful that it impacted the way she saw her world even in her last rite of passage. The first hand experience of witnessing God gave her the courage, strength and insight to go on. She had always believed in God and Jesus and as she looked up to the sky that day, she said out loud; "Dear Lord you and I both know you have lots of special beautiful children in this world and you and I both know I am not one of them. Please Lord, just put my light out."

She was out of body and floating towards the light and once she reached the Light of God, the peace, joy, freedom, and bliss does not begin to describe this wondrous experience. She remembers begging God to let her stay but the answer was, "No" and she was told telepathically she wasn't finished yet. Finished with what? She was not sure but being in God's waiting room she felt she was finally doing the work she came here to do.

Ailill knew she needed to be rigorously honest concerning her failures, missteps, and character defects along with her successes, joys, emotional pain and accomplishments. Even at the risk of being called Miss Van Aster and Goodie Two Shoes. Her critical parent voices still echoed their opinions in her mind.

Over the years Ailill begged for her family to give her another chance. She so desperately wanted them to meet their sober mother who at the time had twenty-six years sobriety. In her mind, that was her true amends and she was not the mother they remembered growing up with.

She kept all her correspondence with her family over the years. The following memos were kept secret as her begging and pleading to make amends was not talked about. The only things they held onto were the ongoing stories of their horrific childhood. These patterns of character assignation, blaming, and keeping score with the past resulted in years of estrangement and separations between family members. Ailill's part in the separations was her pattern of running away and hiding. Unfortunately it added to her children's sense of abandonment as an absentee parent. She knew her daughter Kaitlyn was still energetically living life after her diagnosis with cancer because she followed her on Facebook.

Ailill sent this e-mail November 11, 2010

"Dear Kaitlyn & Family:
Christmas is near and I would like to invite you and your family including Bob & Helena (her mother and father-in-law) to one day of sharing. I promise the menu will include:
No conversation of past hurts and sorrows.
No one else will be invited unless you request it.
The main course will be just the joy of being together.
I love you and I miss you. Please think about this and let me know the day and time if you can find it in your heart for just one day I would be forever grateful.
All My Love
Mom"

Her oldest daughter's Brianna response: November 16, 2010

Notice as you read Ailill's daughter's letter the depth of her pain in sharing her sister's cancer diagnosis. Ailill's daughters were less than a year apart in age. They were closer than twins. Brianna was a medical professional and assisted her sister with insurance problems, medication questions, and medical contacts. She wanted to protect her sister in every way possible. Ailill realized later that she was the safe one to attack, blame, hold responsible and Brianna needed to vent her anger and pain. In an unexplainable way, looking back she realized how this letter was an alternative to compromise because she was excluded from their lives at the time.

Brianna wrote: "Your daughter Kaitlyn called me today and was so upset that she could hardly talk. I don't know if you recall that your daughter was diagnosed with terminal cancer earlier this year. And

58

you send her an email asking her to go to YOU for Christmas, and it would make YOU very grateful. But I need to tell you because she doesn't have the strength to, that she is just not physically or emotionally strong enough to go to anyone right now. She is in the fight of her life, trying to stay alive and spend as much time with her kids as possible. Your email did not even ask how you are. How is your family dealing with having a Mommy/Wife that is gone every other week in ICU getting high dose IL-2 Kemo? She goes to ICU because the high dose of IL-2 chemo therapy kills almost half of the patients from the treatment alone. Nor did your email mention anything along the lines of: I am SORRY, I wasn't there for you when you had to go to ICU alone, and you couldn't even drive home because your eyes were swollen shut, and your heart rate dropped so low, they didn't know if you were going to make it to your next treatment. I am SORRY, I wasn't there when your fever got so high your entire body blistered leaving every inch of your body scabbed, and the kids were scared of their Mommy. I am SORRY; I wasn't there for you when you were told you are going to die from this disease. If you do this horrific treatment, at best you might have a few more months with your kids. I am SORRY, I wasn't there for you when you were put on hospice and a nurse came to your home every day to give you meds, check your vitals, and provide you comfort measures because medically there isn't anything else they can do but give you multiple pain meds, so your life is like being in a coma every day.

I am SORRY; you are going through life with a hole in your neck so the doctors have a main line access to your arteries because your veins all blew out from the chemo. I know you need a Mom right now more than ever in your short life, and I am sorry, I could not be by your side and love you in sickness and in health for nothing: and with no strings attached. That's what my sister needs!! Not to go to YOU, and sit around and psycho rap about nothing. May God help you, he blessed you with 3 children, and you were so blessed in life you got to see them ALL grow up. Just try to imagine what my sister is facing without family support. I love her so much, I would give my life to save her, so she can be there to see her kids go to high school, get a driver's license, have their first date, graduate, start college, all the joys of the kids firsts in life, we have been there to see our kids go through all she is being robbed of. For the life of me I do not, nor will I ever understand why you don't run to her side, and just be with her, and love her with no invitations, no words, for whatever time she has. Love does not need to be invited or spoken, love is actions. So I am going to graciously decline for all of us and her family for Christmas. She needs to focus all of her time and energy on fighting cancer, and just doesn't have anything left to contribute to one-sided relationships. I would like to ask you to please leave her alone, these bull shit emotional games have always been exceptionally hard for her, and now it is life-threatening to her well being, and her families well being. They have been through enough hurt this year to last them all a lifetime. So please respect their wishes. Thank you for your understanding and cooperation".

These letters were placed in the pages amongst Ailill diary. She was repeatedly reminded of her failure and shortcomings throughout her life. Ailill kept all her letters, all her memories of the good, bad ugly as precious mementos of her life's journey. This particular one was a final curtain call, or so she thought at the time because when her daughter was diagnosed with terminal cancer and she was told by Kaitlyn and everyone else how she was not allowed to come to the hospital to be by her side, devastated, overwhelmed and distressed; but that doesn't begin to explain this mothers total heartbreak. Another reason she is glad to include all the bad and the ugly as part of her story is to validate how such deep scars can and eventually did transcend into stars in this family's saga.

Ailill and Kaitlyn were reunited a few weeks later and they shared the next thirty-six months openly loving, sharing, and reminiscing all the challenges, horrors and pain they had caused one another. The forgiveness, love, and reunion was a walk through heavens gate even before Kaitlyn got there. Kaitlyn Norse didn't make her transition until January 18, 2013. What mother would not want to settle the score and claim who she really was. Ailill was the one with her during Hospice, taking care of her toddler grandchildren, cooking, buying the school clothes, laundry etc.? Kaitlyn and her family would come to grandmother's house for extended periods of time and Ailill had the honor and privilege of staying with her daughter weeks at a time. Her oldest daughter, Brianna to this day didn't know. Ailill honored her youngest daughter's wishes to not tell her sister when she was at Ailill's house or when she was with Kaitlyn at her house. Kaitlyn didn't want her sister to be angry at her. Ailill was repeatedly in the same town and couldn't go visit her other daughter and grandchildren. Kaitlyn did not want to look weak in her sister's eyes. Brianna had shared with her mother and sister that she understood that Kaitlyn needed a mother but that she did not.

Ailill's silence and agreement to all those secrets has only contributed to endorsing her reputation of absentee mother and grandmother. By writing about Ailill's diary it is my hope that her family members will come to understand the tight rope she agreed to walk as she strived for balance. Ailill did not have the opportunity or the ability to share her truth with her oldest daughter, Brianna because her grief is still so intense with the loss of her sister and best friend. How could she after the fact add to her daughter's loss?

She knew, firsthand how devastating survivor's guilt can be. It is truly amazing how it took Ailill facing her own death before she was able write about and shed light on her own limitations, successes and triumphs. Her youngest daughter, Kaitlyn and Ailill had a long good-bye and they had cleared up all the past drama. In fact Ailill wrote volumes about how this experience will forever be," The most glowing pure experience of forgiveness and love you can imagine". Ailill wrote how she wanted everyone to see the power in honesty, the willingness to be venerable and take the opportunity she was taking, even if it was only in the silence of her diary. She wanted to shout out loud how she did in the end become successfully the best mom anyone could want. Kaitlyn gave her that gift and told her so.

With a bit of luck by helping Ailill share her story I can take the sting out of her past reputation. She suspected that the mother bashing was still going on behind her back but she didn't care anymore. She was grateful because she recognized for the first time how this pattern of communicating gave her daughters a sense of bonding through all their own pain of abandonment. In summary of her tragic heart breaks Ailill often wrote: "All things work together for good, not sometimes, maybe or some things but, ALL is perfect in this imperfect world."

While Ailill was staying with her youngest daughter, Kaitlyn all those months during her illness her son, Dean and her three grandsons came for a visit. Her middle grandson, Ryder stopped his grandmother in the hall and tearfully shared with her that he just couldn't believe in God anymore. Her son's family is devout Christians, they went to church every Sunday and their church family was their social focus and became their true spiritual family. Ryder said: "How can I believe in a loving God who would take my Aunt away from my cousins who are only three and four years old?" Her daughter, Kaitlyn overheard him from her bedroom. She loudly said: "Mom, come here and bring the boys with you." When all of them were standing at her bedside, she said: "I know now there is a true and loving God. I have found a personal relationship with Jesus. God allowed me to pull the cancer card as I would have died from my drinking. I also found that I have the most loving mother in the world and I didn't know it all the time I was growing up." Ailill's grandson was so moved that he wrote a story about his Aunts words and won an award for his essay. Ryder read this essay in front of an assembly at his high school. His essay resulted in the teachers, janitors and staff taking up a collection and awarded Kaitlyn and her family a trip to Disneyland.

Ailill wrote in naked vulnerability because she wanted and needed to meet her real self. These letters are the love of her middle daughter, Brianna and her affirmations and success in her own recovery. Ailill had lived long enough to see her family members turn their scars into stars.

Ailill wanted her family, friends, and relatives and everyone else to remember not to nurse your resentments even when they are based in fact. Our wounds may be screaming at us out loud but it hurts us more if we point fingers at one another while so many are pointed back to us.

September 2009 her oldest daughter wrote:

"Hi, I wanted to tell you something that I have never shared with you. I thought of it when you had shared with me, about going to each of us kids at night and being close to us in spirit. I have never told you this, but every single day when I am working, I thank God for allowing me to work at home. And in my prayers, I always thank God for my Mom. When my husband was in jail for domestic violence, the kids and I came to stay with you for a while. You taught me how to use a computer. I could not even control the mouse, and you, very patiently sat with me, for hours, you showed me how to control the mouse by playing games and then onto other programs. It took a long time; I was never a fast learner. And while we were on the computer we were making your famous spaghetti sauce, with a bay leaf in it. Which by the way, I have never been able to make spaghetti sauce even close to that. If I could I would have bottled it and sold it at the supermarket. It is the best in the world!

And now because of you, I can make a living on the computer. Like I have told you before, even though I never tell you, we are closer, more alike, and more connected in more ways than physically. I know because I feel it every day. And there is a sense of peace. I just thought I would share that with you. Talk to you soon.
Love,"

Love is the answer. The ups, downs, low points, high points are the spiral of each of us learning how to become the best human we can be. I am compelled, as is Ailill, to share the ugly with the beautiful. Without the contrast and reading between the lines the truth of the hard road to success would only be a path of unbelievable destruction.

Ailill's daughters, for twenty-four years needed to "mother bash". She felt she had earned it in that they ended up in a very prestigious reform school in Utah. It was supposed to have counseling for adolescents, nurturing, and life skills for anorexia, bulimia, addictions, and depression due to broken families. Kaitlyn and Brianna spent over two years in this institution because of the decisions Ailill made and their experience was that their mother had ruined their lives. Her youngest daughter, Kaitlyn was over 5' 10" tall and weighed only eighty-three pounds and Ailill was hard-pressed to find size zero, even in children's shops. Her middle daughter was on the brink of quitting school and her friends were twenty-seven years old, just getting out of detox, when she was only sixteen. Ailill agreed to allow them to go because in her brokenness due to he alcoholism she just knew that anyone could give them more than she could. She had accepted the fact that she had failed as a person and knew she was bankrupt in every area of life.

63

Brianna shared with her mother a funny story about the brokenness of their lives at that time. A few years back she was in counseling over a marital conflict with her husband. The counselor asked her if her mother loved her, was nurturing and encouraging. Her answer was: "Are you kidding?" "When my mom divorced my Dad all four of us had issues with substance abuse at the same time. The only difference was that my Mom was the only one old enough to have a drivers license." Ailill still laughs out loud when she thinks of how her family's sense of humor has allowed all of them to re-see their tragedies.

Ailill kept this letter as another beautiful gift of her daughter's forgiveness and how Brianna continues to turn her scars into stars. Her daughter's journey in her own recovery is shared here. Her description of incomprehensible demoralization is beautiful. She is currently working in the field of recovering addicts /alcoholics so Ailill and I both know she will approve of us sharing her experience, strength and hope for future generations and those still struggling on their own journeys.

"Hi Mom
I have wanted to talk to you something for weeks now. I don't remember how the conversation got started but. She (her sister) did mention that she was still very upset that you had not made it up there, because she could not wait to "Show Mom my house that I bought, and show Mom all that I have accomplished in spite of her"..And then she said wouldn't you be pissed if Mom did that to you? I said the old me would have been, but believe it or not, I understand Mom more now than I have ever understood her in my life. She asked what does that mean. I told her that it's not about buying houses; it's not about how much money you have. Maybe Mom didn't come because she is still too hurt. Did you ever think about that?

I told her that I was taking methadone, and have not had any narcotics in 9 months, and now that my head is clear, life just makes more sense, and my life is the clearest it has ever been.

I then told her that I had been thinking allot about a year ago, and that whole scenario. I told my sister, to put it in a nutshell, Mom saw that we were fighting and competing over her, and she took the toy away that we were fighting over. I then talked to her, for the first time, about how I never felt like it was a competition, and she admitted to me it was and she would do anything to win. I told her I felt like her and my relationship was very strained over the past year, and how hurt I was that she sabotaged every relationship that has ever meant anything to me. And she did the same to my brother She proceeded to tell me I didn't know him, and he sets people up to use them, and blah, blah.

I just told her I know my brother allot more than she thinks I do and he and I have spent some time talking, and that is not at all his agenda. I did tell her that my brother does not allow anyone to talk about anyone else because he views gossip to be like murder of another person, and he would never say gossip about her or any of us in a negative way. I also told her that I loved her, and I can only hope and pray that she focus on her little ones right now, they need their mommy more now than ever. I also told her "time outs" are not "I don't love you", it's just a reflection time, and regrouping for everyone and that is OK and can be healthy. I told her it is not forever, and love does heal all, and when the time is right everything will work itself out, and she will know when the time is right because love is not hard or painful. She did not hear me, she just became very angry, and said, "Are you talking to Mom again?"I told her "No," and I also made it very clear to her that she will never know who, or what, or when I am in a relationship with anyone.

That trust has been destroyed, and it still hurts, and I am not over it yet. And I tried to explain to her that I want to stop this hurtful cycle in our family, and I also need a "time out". She said she had to go, and I have never heard a word from her since. So, I wanted to let you know because I am not going to say another word about her. I do love her very much, but she is not there yet. I wish her all the best and I will pray for her and those babies every single day!

We don't talk about it in my house anymore, and we are just focusing on our reunited healthy and loving relationships. I do feel like this is our time. And by our time, I mean mother and daughter, and grandmother and grandchildren. The kids love you so much, and we have a lot of lost time to make up for. How is this for a novel? If you scroll down and look at your email and then mine, Oh My Gosh. And to think we spent 9 hours on the phone, and we still have so much to say. I think, no I know I got that trait from you. I love you so very much. And I am the luckiest girl in the world to have you as my Mom. I thank God every day for the second chance. Oh, one more thing...I hope the part where you said let us not do the fight and flight thing again. I can't believe that was me. I don't even remember what I fought about, do you? I was such a bitch, but I swear it is all gone; it just lifted and flew away. Do you know that when you fight all the time, and when you are a bitch every day it is impossible to be happy? And it's exhausting. OK, I am done. I can't type anymore, I am going to bed. I do love you with all of my heart. I hope you sleep well tonight.

All my love forever,
Your Daughter"

Ailill's son, Dean's take on the years of estrangement and hatefulness has been; "Mom, you forgive and forget and go back and try, struggling again, to get my sisters to love and accept you but what happens is that you get in the ring with the bear and the bear eats you every time."

I love that all of Ailill's family members have such a wonderful sense of humor and the obvious gift of healing it has on each of them.

Journaling was the main therapeutic healing tool for Ailill as she was in God's waiting room. She discovered through looking closely at her life that it allowed for her to be the closest she had ever been to the truth of her Soul. These are some of the things that she had written to herself over the years: "Be open to surprises. Get back to your center and always hold yourself accountable. I will practice what I preach; I will walk my walk and by doing this I give me back to myself. Believe in your intuition and I can trust that I am on the right path. I am learning through joy and pain and remember to always return to love. The awesome power of love and forgiveness is God Godding through me. I am willing to learn through this process because I am here for soul growth. What I am looking for I am looking with, God is as close as my own breath."

Ailill wrote about her quiet times. "I can get quiet and listen to the still small voice inside me as I write to myself saying: Even though I don't know it, I can't be off my path, especially when I've had my life focus fixated on something that didn't belong to me. When I feel like I've lost something I have to remind myself, no judgment, no expectations. I know that I've taken a left turn off my path when I do or say certain things that are a betrayal of me. Today, when I feel like I've taken a detour I can remind myself that I do not have to betray myself anymore."

Through meditation and prayer, she was beginning to understand that her negative thinking was costing her the loss of her personal power. Compromise was not betraying herself. Choosing to live in Grace she experienced holiness because that is the only time that she learned to withdraw from her five senses. Rational thought no longer owned her because when she listened to her ego voices they would usually tell her lies.

One of her favorite daily prayers was asking God to hover over her, "God please enter where you already abide." As Ailill aged one of the most wonderful freedoms experienced was giving up her right to know. She continued to seek guidance through prayer on what she needed to change and what she needed to accept. When she experienced confusion it usually was when she was not being honest with herself and when she was trying to control something that she truly was not able to control. For instance, the last year in bed she waffled between whether she was being a quitter and giving into hopelessness or did she need to accept the things she could not change?

These are the times when she needed to remind herself that God is the law and order of things good. The words I share with you from her journaling over the years is an invitation for us all to protect our possibility of experiencing God's love in everything and everywhere.

As her family knew she was a fervent, devoted reader. This year during her convalescence she read over one hundred books. Be careful what you pray for, she never had the time to read, pray, meditate and paint as much as she wanted to. Now she had all the time in the world.

Ailill had extensively studied comparative religions since she was ten years old. What she knew is that no religion has a monopoly on love. She believed we can't be separated from God, whether we know it or not. In her counseling, teaching, and writings she helped others to see when they were walking towards love or towards fear. She believed that she was more afraid of success than failure. The key to happiness is the decision to be happy.

Ailill wrote about how she used to believe it came from things outside of herself like the perfect job, mate or family when she finished school, etc. It was never anything on the outside of her that brought true and lasting happiness it was in the connecting to the energy of everyone and everything beyond labels and ideas. Some call it a Soul, the eternal part of each of us that is created in the image of our one true creator, she called God. The longest hardest part of her life was the eighteen inches between the heart and her head. I believe this applies to each and every one of us. It is only when we are out of our minds and into our heart language that all of us experience truth and happiness.

She wrote to her loved ones in heaven regularly and she honestly rejoiced when she could remind herself that eternity knows no present, no yesterday and all that ever existed or will exist is in the NOW. She got holy Goosebumps when she recognized how to choose to be falling into Grace. She allowed it to be here and now; it is here now, and she learned how to open her heart to know that.

Ailill believed that as her loved ones shared their generational suffering it was the universal teacher that was looking for resolution. Every one of us; down deep within ourselves, we know that our direct investigation of spirit doesn't have to have a name, religion, or even an idea of good or bad. It is what it is and we can choose to celebrate the Grace of a new day. One infinite all-inclusive presence is our connection to God. Ailill did consider herself a Christian and believed that the Lord Jesus being man and God is our savior and redeemer of our human sins. She also believed that Christ is not Jesus' last name but the Christ that lives in all. For over fifty years whenever she was with a patient, client, friend, or anyone, she would say a prayer to herself. "May the Christ in me speak to the Christ in you and please get Ailill out of the way."

I read this statement many times in Ailill's journals and in her diary. "Today's Battles, Tomorrow's Strength"

She believed the truth of the story, today's battles and tomorrow's strength, originated with Jesus.

Matthew 6:34 (KJV)
Therefore do not worry about tomorrow, for tomorrow will worry about itself. Each day has enough trouble of its own.

Ailill wrote her views about this scripture. God supplies all the strength we need. We have been given what He's called us to do. But He rations this strength much the same way he rationed manna to the children of Israel. He provides sufficient strength each day for the challenge of that day.... and that day only. This strength doesn't carry over from one day to the next. You either use it or lose it. She learned that God will not give her enough strength for the confrontations, obligations, and challenges of next week, next month, or next year. This strength will be deposited in our account precisely when we need it, and not a moment before. And that's all she needed for now.

As I review her meanderings through her journal I am visualizing her family reading about her life even fifty years from now. The reason I say this is the first two books she wrote was with the vision of her books being used in prisons, juvenile halls, and group homes. Ailill's books were rejected because they said there was too much God in them. The assistant warden of a local prison said that our prison system isn't ready for the solutions she presented because it is a multi-million dollar business and they are not ready to entertain a real solution. Her books were written as a self-discovery through journaling and how to connect to the answers that already abide in each one of us.

Hey Guys, if she is fifty years ahead of her time, please remember to read her books again and notice how truth resonates with each of us as we grow and glow in the presence of the God who resides inside of us as spirit and soul.

Ailill loved what Albert Einstein said: "We will never find a solution if we continue to look for it in the minds that created the problem."

The experience of not allowing for healing to come through faith was one of Ailill's continuous nagging voices throughout her writings. God is left out of our schools, our government and religious superiority is still an issue even against all knowledge to the contrary. She talked about how she can honestly say she found that amazing when we are so educated and still choose to live in the problem of best, most and better. We are educated, living in a society of remarkable technology and we still choose not to play well with others. Our underlying motto is run harder, go faster and do more. What is happening to integrity, grace and unity especially when we know we only have to do unto others what we want for ourselves? Kindness is just a little love we leave behind us as we trudge the road to happy destiny. Curious don't you agree?

Ailill was intrigued by imagination. What would happen if we turned the microscope just a little bit and believed all negative energy was just looking for a solution? Today we live in a society where science is giving us proof of the spiritual truths we used to only be able to hypothesize about and imagine. Why is it we still choose to turn a blind eye?

I concur with Albert Einstein who said: "**Imagination** is more important than knowledge. For knowledge is limited, whereas **imagination** embraces the entire world, stimulating progress, giving birth to evolution."

Connections

Chapter 8

All Trials and Tribulations Have Value

"Trials and tribulations offer us a chance to make reparation for our past faults and sins. On such occasions, the Lord comes to us like a physician to heal the wounds left by our sins. Tribulation is the divine medicine."
Saint Augustine

This is our shared journey through crisis and chaos to unconditional love.

Ailill's reframing of her past relationships came to the surface during her time in God's waiting room because she realized she silently spoke her soulful truth. It was easy to share who she was to everyone but her family. Ailill's life journey only happened in the privacy of her journals and diary over the years. It was these reminders that fueled her courage and acceptance in how she worked through her dark times. In reviewing her old journal entries she realized it wasn't about digging up the past but about honoring how she survived the past and the pain. Shining a light on her hidden pain was difficult at best but she found help from these valuable quotes that she saved in her diary. She copied them down and re-read them over the years. She found comfort again and again when she consulted her favorite pearls of wisdom.

"We face up to awful things because we can't go around them. The sooner you say 'Yes, it happened,' the sooner you can get on with your own life." – Annie Proulx

"Prosperity is a great teacher; adversity is greater." William Hazlitt

"You need to spend time crawling alone through shadows to truly appreciate what it is to stand in the sun." Shaun Hick

"Without the burden of afflictions, it is impossible to reach the height of grace. The gift of grace increases as the struggle increases."St. Rose of Lima

Ailill was contemplating taking a leap of faith in that she was challenging the generational rule of Don't Talk, Don't Trust and Don't Feel. It is through the personal portraits and memories that she came to know that everyone who is still experiencing the pain and hurt of navigating their own life that she saw once again that nothing was ever wasted. Every soul on this planet has experienced pain and challenges. She was going to share her personal letters with all her amazing family members and validate for herself as she struggled for emotional stability in her infirmed state.

Her life review illustrated the depth of pain and destruction addictions played in clouding and denying everyone's true selves. She reflected on how her families started out only trying to self medicate their pain through chemicals and in blaming each other. She made a decision that she did not want to waste time in this last chapter of her life story. She was ready to let it all hang out. She prayed that she would not expose any personal confidence when she shared her stories. The gift she wanted to give to everyone was honesty. Own her struggles and she hoped that her loved ones were ready and willing to talk about it; to say it like it is.

For Ailill it was never about hatred or blame but only unconditional love. She intended to praise the heroines and heroes of her life story. Between herself, her sisters and brother, and their combined twenty-eight grandchildren, many are still estranged from one another because of the rampant addictions that have been inherited and handed down from the O'Sullivan clan.

She talked about their deep heartfelt struggles and their successes to illustrate that if all of us never give up and never give in we can heal with such amazing Grace. Love always wins in the end. Ailill discovered that alcoholism had been in their family for five generations, so the O'Sullivan clan came by it honestly. Her proof was when she took her parents to Ireland for their twenty-fifth wedding anniversary in 1974. They visited the cemetery in Cork County, where her ancestors were buried. A distant cousin, who was taking them on the tour, explained why Ailill's great, great-grandfathers tombstone read; "Here Lays This Soul in Purgatory". Their tour guide told them it was because he was a hopeless, helpless alcoholic. At first, Ailill was aghast but upon reflection she realized that five generations later the O'Sullivan clan is now living a new legacy of love and hope, which in turn honors all their ancestors spanning over 500 years.

William Shakespeare wrote: "All the world's a stage, and all the men and women merely players: they have their exits and their entrances, and one man in his time plays many parts, His acts being seven stages".

Ailill was determined to expand on her goal to share how we all find the sacred in the ordinary and how true awareness is usually disguised as trials and tribulations.

Proverbs: 31 (KJV)
"God draws his straightest lines from life's greatest difficulties to our deepest joys."

Ailill described the experience of being in God's waiting room as like looking in one of those magnifying mirrors that highlights every imperfection. Fine facial hairs look forest thick, the skin pores appear as large craters. But she found value in looking closely, even if those magnifying mirrors were scary.

This distorted view was how she saw herself for many years. She wrote in her diary how she got to the point where she no longer even recognized herself. The perverse opinions of those who were supposed to love her caused her to see herself in a warped mirror. For decades she only saw herself through their perspective. Her daughters told her she had ruined their lives, and they had 1,000 derailed memories of how she did everything wrong.

Imagine waking up one day and seeing a monstrosity reflected in your mirror, and believing it is the real you for over forty years. In reviewing her journals, she recognized the constant blame and accusations of twisted memories. She realized her daughters have made hating her their life's work. Twenty years ago she might have listened with some sympathy, but as the years go by she had to wonder exactly what were her adult children getting out of all this hating. They did admit to her once that they recognized they were haters but also enjoyed it and they were proud of it. Ailill finally realized that if any of their grievances were actually real, they would not be worth obsessing over even for a week, let alone decade after decade.

Reviewing her life, Ailill can honestly say that there was never one day of her adult children's lives (now in their 50's); that she woke up with the thought, "How can I mess up the lives of my children today?" The only conclusion she came to was that her daughters especially enjoyed hating her. It somehow gave them some sort of excuse and validation for justifying their existence. The time and energy that her daughters put into their fantasies are still puzzling even now at the end of her life's journey. It's clear to her today that most of it is, in fact is fantasy. So what she realized today, which she didn't recognize for the last 40 years is there's not a lot she could do about it. They had a very long pity party and she became their scapegoat.

Ugly memories:

For example:

"Dear Mom, I have been thinking a lot about your email, and what you said. You ask me to be honest with you and speak from my heart so that is what I'm going to do. This mother-daughter relationship has been by far the hardest on me throughout my adult life. And to be honest with you I don't like myself very much when I am in a "relationship" with you. It is very destructive for me emotionally. We all are screaming to be loved and cared about it, and our family (the people who are supposed to love us no matter what) take a "time out". I have cried out countless times for your love and attention more times than I could count, and you were never available. I have learned to cope with life on my own, and yes it has made me a hard ass bitch. But it was my way of getting through life struggles on my own. I am with my little sister as well as with my kids trying a different approach. I hope you find what you're looking for in life, and find peace and happiness with no regrets, and don't worry my sister and I will be just fine, we always have been. I do agree with my sister that it's best if you don't contact either of us anymore, it just causes more hurt. And neither of us has time to deal with anymore hurt, our plates are full. Take Care, with love"

Ailill painted The Eye of Judgment in 2008 when she was being attacked by her daughters. She could only see herself as an alien, her heart was broken wide open, the family tree has alcoholism and masks. She needed boots to trudge through the muck and mire of hatred. She was caged by the opinions of those who were supposed to love her. She titled it the Eye of Judgment which pierced her heart and chained her soul. She felt locked in without a prayer. Sometimes pictures are worth a 1000 words. She cried rivers in her grief for many years. Her heart was upside down and she tried to hold on to her broken heart but her tender sensitive heart had wings and would fly away. Ailill had never displayed this painting to anyone before showing it to me.

Eye of Judgment

When she healed enough to begin to forgive herself she wrote in her journal: "I still knew that healing the wreckage of my past was the most traumatic for my adult children. I realized that their forgiveness might be impossible." Ailill shared with me that her naked exposure here was freeing. She only corresponded in private letters and e-mails because her part, even in recovery was to just turn the other cheek. Through prayer and trying so desperately to take the high road, she hoped forgiveness would happen in time. Now Ailill realizes she entertained magical thinking rather than verbally, emotionally and physically standing up for herself. The outcome is that because of her silence, being meek, crawling under the rug and hiding, she provided more ammunition for slander and ridicule. In secret, only in the privacy of her mind and her journal did she plead her case; state her pain. Only through the consequence of being in God's waiting room did she decide to hold her head high now that she was looking at the end of her life.

Ailill shared openly with me about the correspondence from her adult children during the time where no matter what she did or said she was confronted with so much fault-finding, name-calling and blame. She had to apply tough love practices for her own sanity as well as for the well-being of her adult children. Sometimes the deepest, strongest love is the toughest.

The repercussion of all that had gone on in the past was the knowledge that she was estranged from her grandchildren. They grew up hearing stories and complaints from their parents; accusations against their mother for the unrequited nurturing/love, they fantasized about. The result being that her grandchildren don't expect her to show up at weddings etc. because they are used to hearing how she never supported any of them.

In her journal entries, even as of 2019, she recognized how she continued to feel the same. She understood their perceptions of what they call her psychobabble. The difference today is that the ones that can hear do. The ones that dismiss truth in favor of denial, minimizing, rationalizing and justifying still do. The truth will set us free. The only problem with that statement is that everyone's truth can be astonishingly different.

"Good Morning Sweetheart:
I know I have been neglectful due to a lifetime of conditioning to give 130%, but my craziness is that it has never been from an ego place but just an attempt to feel normal. Unfortunately, or fortunately, I am not sure which I passed that trait on to my children. I can't begin to tell you how proud I am of your success in your life. You have remained a committed, loving, dutiful mother, found a way to support everyone, never let pain, troubled abusive marriage, addictions, or finances stop you. Your challenges have all been met with courage, fortitude, and yes your anger has also been a great motivator that you had to have, as it is a powerful energy. I just want you to understand that I have always known that you do what you do to survive and you have done it very well. Both you and your sister have lived your lives insisting on experiencing everything life had to offer, and then some. I also knew and still know that everything has its own time. I am so glad it is our time now. We have both been praying and waiting for this to happen for a long time."

This is an example of what her children call Psychobabble:

"I am going to share a sacred belief that I have today. If there are truly no mistakes in God's world, that means you and I have finished whatever karmic debt we have had with abusive relationships in any form. We are finally free, our lessons have been learned and by the laws of attraction, and cause and effect we have loving, supportive and encouraging partners. In other words, I am always telling grandpa I have paid my dues and the fruits of all of our labors, hardship, and rejection are now over, isn't that wonderful? What is more wonderful is that now you can mentor that to your children, my grandchildren, they are learning also of a better more loving way of life. Anyway, my thoughts of gratitude were just too awesome this morning. I, like you, have found my daily prayers of gratitude are by far the greatest remedy of all life's challenges and upsets.
My entire Love Mom"

Ailill wanted so badly to heal the separation of sisters and brothers and family members. So she continues to work at mending fences. She acknowledged to me that when I write her story it may look like I'm hanging out her laundry for everyone to see, digging up her dirty past, shame, guilt, and emotional pain of the O'Sullivan family. I admit that this is exactly what I am doing because documenting the intensity of all their scars is the only way you will see how brightly their stars shine as this clan is breaking the chains of a multi-generational legacy. Their heroism and fortitude is an example for all of us.

Ailill openly shared with me how she had been shamed, embarrassed, and at times stigmatized. Even today, years later, she fears retribution and liability. Some of this may have been deserved at one time, but today her story is one of success. It is a story of hope, support and recovery. I share her intimate tale so that you and everyone else can hear the human side of this addictive disease, of its treacherous grip, and of the freedom and confidence from which the O'Sullivan clan has emerged and continues to emerge from this terrifying and devastating illness.

Ailill confessed to me how therapeutic this exercise has been for her. She is hell-bent on denying the legacy of an absentee parent or grandmother and being constantly accused of being the main source of abandonment in her family's history. She needed to clarify with future generations how easy it is to be identified by other people's opinions of you. If it walks like a duck, talks like a duck, it's a duck. She believed she was that duck because others said so. I feel blessed by the opportunity to share her story, as an overview of her life.

"Good Morning Dear Daughters.
I miss you so very much! I was wondering if you had any suggestions on how we might be able to heal our relationships and what you think it would take to never repeat this pattern.
I look forward to hearing from you.
My entire Love Mom"

This is the memo she received in response:

"Ailill Star, Your path of destruction runs long and deep. This is the last communication I plan on ever having with you for the rest of our lives.
I have spent most of my life not knowing much about you. Over the last eight years, I allowed you back in my life just to be abandoned one more time. Stupid Me, I guess people never do change. You make Mary O'Sullivan win Mother of the Year

I WILL NEVER ALLOW THIS TO HAPPEN AGAIN!
And I quote your son "the next time I see my Mother will be at her Memorial Service", see you then
God Bless your Soul"

Any attempt on Ailill's part, hoping for forgiveness and healing just ended up becoming fodder, yet one more opportunity for aggression and denunciation. She was told she was too sensitive or it was just words. The truth is that emotional rape happens often in estranged families. Words can kill. Forgiveness is wonderful, even achievable, but being able to forget is wholly a different matter. I have a couple of friends who practice Shamanism using healing techniques for soul retrieval. The words, emotional rape, and character assignations take pieces of the soul away leaving gaping holes in your spirit.

Romans 1:29 (KJV)
"They have become filled with every kind of wickedness, evil, greed, and depravity. They are full of envy, murder, strife, deceit, and malice. They are gossips."

Gossip can prove to be worse than murder. It is then Ailill realized how the pattern of abandonment and punishment is still alive and active in her family relationships. I am going to go out on a limb here because I realize Ailill has some family members who will attack her and hold her responsible, blame and abandon her again for sharing this story. I think we both came to the conclusion that the truth was they had already abandoned her. She asked herself "What and who am I protecting? Is this pattern still my Karma? If it's true that we do reap what we sow I must still have some accountability that I am not seeing yet."

Ailill's granddaughter, Makenna got married last month. When she spoke with Makenna she indicated that it was very important to her that her grandmother attend her wedding. Ailill called to tell her she was still too weak and sick to attend. Makenna was so surprised because she didn't even know her grandmother was sick. For the last twelve months, her daughter, Brianna never mentioned to her children that their grandmother was ill or possibly dying. In an angry moment with her bride to be daughter, Brianna told her that her daughter, Makenna that she should understand because after all, her grandmother had never supported her or anyone else in anything.

Ailill recognized this scenario. The truth had to be kept from her grandchildren because the underlying fear was that during an innocent conversation the truth might be found out. The basic instinct was to protect exposing all the history and the fantasies. The blame game was afoot!

Can you imagine Ailill's total disbelief when her then twenty-six-year-old granddaughter came to visit and brought a bottle of wine? She asked grandpa if he had a wine opener and he said, "Yes, I am sure we have one somewhere". It was then that her daughter, Brianna went up to Makenna and told her that her grandmother was a recovering alcoholic. Brianna responded with surprise saying she didn't know that. Ailill was in recovery for thirty years, a drug & alcoholic counselor. She wrote two books about recovery and her granddaughter had no idea. I hope my readers are beginning to see why she constantly questioned her view of her own distorted mirror image. It validates how true it is that the most important people in her life didn't know her. Problem solved, now you have a story telling you who Ailill is, what her soul, heart, truth and healing looks like. Ailill's life's work has been dedicated to helping others while her family remains in judgment. Although she has helped so many others over the years with healing, her family still remains a mystery to her. She realizes today that her silence wasn't golden, just stupid.

Ailill agreed to let me share her life story because she saw it as an exercise for her in soul retrieval. I am going to tell her truth. Over the last thirty years, she had kept in touch with all her grandchildren through their parents. She had followed them closely all their lives, but once removed, via the third person. She shared with her daughter, Brianna how that was the only opening she ever had because Brianna was unwilling to share her family. In a conversation later Brianna openly admitted that she was/is unwilling to share her family. Hurtful dysfunction is still alive with that old, don't talk, don't trust, don't feel rule.

The pink elephant is protected and defended in our secrecy and manipulations of the truth. By pulling off the blinders and finally saying what she has needed to say, Ailill is gaining new freedom.

81

Over the years, not being willing to vent, Ailill is now in her last will and testimony, finding an act of new courage.

I am painting a true life scenario of how each of her family members played their part. Ailill knows their association is sacred as they are a true Soul family. We are the teachers and students of one another. Every family in the universe knows the deepest scars can come from our family members. They represent our deepest loves, our greatest desires, and our pains and that is where our sorrows accumulate.

Ailill's AA sponsor for the last fourteen years shared great deal of wisdom and insight with her. Her funeral is only three days away which she was sure that it added to her melancholy and depression the day of this interview. Ailill's sponsor had told her what her part was in the continued dysfunction of her family. Ailill had always had an intense need to heal, fix, and mend by loving too hard. Her sponsor pointed out to her how overzealous she became when family members called in a crisis. When they needed comfort, went to jail, quarreled with each other; through divorce, depression, suicidal ideations, etc. They would share their crisis and then they were gone again. Her sponsor said it was Ailill's intensity for love that after the fact, after dumping all their problems in her lap, they wanted and needed to see her in their rearview mirror. They knew that she knew all their truths and they would run for the exit, once again blaming and abandoning her for all their problems in life.

Ailill does get it. Being a counselor, spiritual teacher, member of AA for 33 years and putting on her white robe climbing to the top of the mountain can be and has been a real turn off for her family. She openly admitted that she couldn't imagine having a relative like her when she was active in her alcoholism and drug addictions. She had to be their worse nightmares come true when they were in her presence.

Her daughter, Kaitlyn shared this truth with her towards the end of her life. She asked her, "Mom, do you understand why I had to hate you all these years?" Ailill did share with her how confusing it was. She said, "Just being in your presence makes me feel like dog (chit). I hate being around anybody who makes me feel bad about me."

82

She would want everyone who reads these words to see the valuable lesson she learned that day. Maybe it truly is just words. In our anger, rage, and character assignations there is shame, low self-esteem and guilt shouted **Out-Loud.** What if it never did have anything to do with us, as we are mirrors to one another? Ailill's sponsor gave her this affirmation and instructed her to read it many times over. When Ailill would get into her self-loathing and rehearsing all the mistakes she had made during her life she would re-read this gift from her sponsor.

I Am Enough

Today, I am enough.
I am smart enough.
Wise enough.
Clever enough.
Resourceful enough.
Able enough.
Confident enough.
I am connected to enough people to accomplish my heart's desire.
I have enough ideas to pull off magic and miracles.
Enough is all I need.
Enough is what I have.
I have more than enough.
As I do all that I can do, I am able to do more and more.
I am excited to be alive. I rejoice and re-choice every day to make
my life better.
I am happy, healthy, prosperous, successful, rich, loving, loved and
beloved.
I am comfortable with myself, so I am comfortable with all others.
I confidently greet each day with a smile on my face and love in
my heart.
Everyone who meets me is warmed by the radiance of my attitude.
I work on my attitude continuously. I read positive, inspiring and
uplifting books.
I associate with friendly, caring, nurturing people who are involved
in doing important things.
The people with whom I associate want more for me than I want
for myself.
The projects with which I am involved WOW my soul.
I am passionately on-purpose to do good, be good and help others
do the same.
I am enough. I have enough. I do enough.

Ailill shared in her real-time moments as it happened to illustrate
that if she could transcend such terrible pain and destruction,
anyone can. Being here in God's waiting room with all of her
memories, please don't misunderstand how she truly honored the
good and for the first time was taking an honest look at the bad.

She was so filled with gratitude and joy for the miles she had
traveled but she would never, ever, want to go back there. It has

taken her facing her demise to challenge her secrets, knowing we all stay as sick as our secrets.

She has exposed the pink elephant that has lived in their living rooms for multiple generations. In reliving her journey she saw where one of the strongest character assets of this Irish Clan is the ability to laugh at themselves. People who learn to laugh at themselves are amused about ninety percent of the time because that is truly how really laughable we are. In Our human condition and facing our addictions will break us so wide open because we finally surrendered. We truly have walked through hell and can now live on the pink cloud of our recovery. Look at all the work Ailill is doing right now. When she does meet Saint Peter at the gate she won't have to waste much time with her Life Review, she is getting it over with early.

Chapter 9

The Natural Beauty of Spirals

"Turn Your World Around and You Can Turn Your World Around"
~ Henry David Thoreau

It has taken a lifetime to learn to see the sacred in the ordinary. Ailill prayed for years, "Thy Will Be Done" and then she proceeded immediately to jump into the driver's seat and run with the whole show. Most of the time she didn't realize she only had power over her territory and road map. She took on the responsibility of everyone else's feelings. Now, she chooses to break her silence and walk out of her shame and guilt.

Ailill asked herself, "What if being here in bed is my new normal? What if this is my new story?" She knew she had become exposed to immeasurable limitations that encompassed her body, mind, and soul. She knew she needed to see her world differently. It took a complete and devastatingly crushing blow to her ego-self to witness her self-righteous superficiality. Ailill had surrendered, given in, faked it, preached it and prayed for guidance and acceptance continually throughout her life. She questioned how she could have attracted such a predicament if thoughts are real things. It has taken a multitude of challenges, crisis, pain, and victories to give her the false impression of seeing herself as a spiritual warrior. Carl Jung coined the phrase, "Wounded Healer", which she identified with because living through her experiences allowed her to comprehend and share her wounds with me. Healing was restored naturally by the formation of scar tissue. Ailill had to launch still another demonstration of courage that she thought she didn't have. Honestly, sharing her journal entries I realized that she was exhausted, looking down a road of total depletion before she discovered that her life had always been a spiral. It cycles as we live and learn and experience that is not about up and down. Using the analogy of climbing a ladder Ailill felt at times like she was going backward. From this vantage point, she saw a destination that she could not reach if she continued to look only at her losses. All physical recourses were gone. She wanted to believe that she had spiritually, mentally, emotionally and physically evolved enough that she thought she was prepared for anything life could throw at her. Ailill had trudged the road of happy destiny before, but now she got to finally come home to herself. By allowing me to write her story she had to give a voice to her unmitigated grief. The most challenging circumstances can catch anyone unaware. She visualized that when she was old and dying that she would do it with dignity and grace. "Ha-ha" that's a laugh! Self-righteous superficiality can look really ugly. The utter panic she experienced when all her wheels fell off was intensely overwhelming.

The spiral is evolving. As she worked so hard to grow her spiritual muscles she discovered that the more important the gift of growth, the greater the resistance. Ouch!

Ailill wondered if she did pray for this. She had always wanted to be the best she could be and leaned heavily on her spirit team for direction. Her goal has always been to be an open vessel in service for the highest best good for herself and others.

Ailill recited to herself on a continuous basis, "I can do all things through Christ who strengthens me." Jesus was and is her mainstay. She held on feverishly to her belief that we were never given more than we could handle. She talked about how much she loved reading the memoirs of Mother Theresa. When one of her followers asked her about this promise, her response was, "Obviously, He has more confidence in us than we do."

Ailill admitted that her grief process always begins with self-sabotage. She needed to find unconventional ways to break through her barriers. Her process is what I am sharing with you now. Divine creativity came forth and has blessed her with a nudge to be a servant of my muse. While she was in bed those 12 months Ailill talked about how automatic writing came so fast and true that she could only choose some of her writings with me due to the massive volumes of enlightenment she was given. There was absolutely nothing left, and then there was something far beyond her wildest imagination. Sometimes her inner self was a voice of questions allowing her to see, really see with a new pair of glasses. She heard, if fear is a factor, then figure out who you are. Ailill knew her Soul was communicating with her, she realized that it was her human self that had lost its resilience but her soul had a strong voice in the quiet of her solitude. Her Higher-self came to her aid and gave her information about how she could rise to the task. She became more herself in the face of adversity. We don't choose what's going to wake us up. The sacred does show up in the most unlikely places. There was a new light that invited her to ignore the dark places in her life and she felt there was a way to flee the darkness, especially her emotional darkness. The richest gifts can be found in the darkest moments. She embraced them and voluntarily went to a place of the unknown. Courage is fear taking action. Ailill asked herself, "How did I learn to be so afraid?" Darkness does not mean we move away from God. It was in the face of death, in the darkness, that she felt a new dazzling, breathtaking energy inviting her to the great expanse of safety. She knew she was learning to walk through the shadows, believing she could navigate in the dark. Ailill practiced staying in the moment instead of clinging to anxiety.

Continuing to be melancholy and downhearted was becoming too much to deal with. She mentally and emotionally knew she didn't want to wait until she experienced how much was too much. Not wanting to run away Ailill went all in. She wondered if she was confined to her bed and that was her new normal, she was reminded that the strength of her spirit knew the way even if she doesn't. Her guardian angels were with her and I sensed that they sat with her while she was sad. She received messages and I wrote them down. You don't have to do anything, just know what is giving you new life right now. I witnessed her opening up to this new space that was showing her a different way of life. Automatically the burning away of unessential's happened, without her doing anything to make it happen. She was allowing and didn't try to manage. She spent hours in meditation and seized upon the promptings to reframe her visions of helplessness. She heard a message saying, "Live with this instead of running from it". She desperately wanted to fulfill her life's purpose. Time was running out and she believed she had fallen short of her goals. She was powerfully being called away and at the same time being called towards something else, something much bigger and stronger than anything she had experienced before. She listened to her heart, "Don't ever give up". When she paid attention to her emotional storms instead of cowering and pulling the covers over her head in despair, she was amazed at the turn of events that made for a much smoother voyage. She had always looked for and sought out what in her mind were large important roles when she was blind to the ordinary. Constantly seeking greatness can be the excuse we use to keep those blinders on.

Ailill's family and friends recognized the change in her and asked her about her new consciousness. Several of them, including me, thanked her for sharing her feelings and thoughts about her last rite of passage with them. Rarely do we have conversations about what it's like to know you are dying. Some of her family members couldn't deal with the visions of her upcoming demise because it was just too terrifying and sad for them to face. One of them actually asked her outright what angel land was really like. They recognized she had taken up a new spiritual residence. Doctors, family, and friends were curious as to where her life force was coming from. All of her vitals and physical weakness were definitely signs she was preparing to cross over.

Most of her doctors kept telling her: "We don't know what's wrong with you Ailill; your insides don't match your outsides. Your vibrant emotional status is contrary to what we see in your test results. There is nothing more we can do for you. You should go home and prepare yourself for the inevitable." The curious part for her was when she did surrender to death. She could truly say she was looking forward to it. It would be the easier way out, but she continued to wake up every morning so she could bless and be blessed for another day. After sharing this with a friend of hers, her friend shared this prayer with her.

A Fervent Prayer
By: Jean Quintana

Dear God,
If I really am chosen; could it be such that is so small a task, as life?

A year ago last August Ailill went with two girlfriends to the Navajo Nation in Arizona to a gathering of healers. Throughout her career, she worked with Native Americans from the Nez Perce reservations in Idaho and Oregon. The messages of the insight she received validated her inner knowing about her life path and purpose. The Elders identified the space she was in. They intuitively knew she was being called to cross over and that she had fulfilled her destiny. Their spirit guides emphasized the fact that she had lived with grace and honor. They graciously thanked her for being a healer and teacher for all of God's people. They didn't know who she was or what she did, but they spontaneously knew and graced her with their insight. She was honored and humbled by their extraordinary gifts of the spirit. The Elders told her that she would be given the choice of being able to stay or go on to the spirit world. Ailill asked;"Where she could be of the greatest service because they stated she had been given the freedom to choose." The Elders said that she had already reached the top of the mountain but if she chose to stay she would still be able to serve. Ailill understood that it did not matter which way she chose, the path was truly blessed either way. Ailill is living that choice today and she is still here to tell me her story.

During her challenging episodes with severe health issues, she wondered, "Is this the day I am going to die?" It's all good though as she knew she had one foot here in her earthly body and thanks to her spirit team who had thinned the veil and everyone who knew her, understood that she walked with them and talked to them constantly by openly participating in her transition. What a wonderful validation this is for Ailill to understand there is nothing she could do to resist her journey and nothing she could do to change her destination. What I learned through Ailill is that none of us are truly victims and life does come to us by some preordained destiny. We signed our contract before entering this earth school. God is in the space between the stars and also in the space between you and me.

The greatest lesson for Ailill and what took her the longest to learn was that she would never be as great as she aspired to be and never as lowly as she thought she was. What I got out of that is we are enough just the way we are. Our greatest task is to trust our walk of faith. Her greatest joy was her compassion. She wanted to abide more in her human heart space because that is where she recognized the total goodness in every one of us. True connectedness has to include learning to praise our shadow side and work hard to maintain our gratitude. Ailill came to realize how fortunate she was to have lost her earthly riches which helped her to find her true wealth. She finally discovered a new understanding that she could absolutely be of service from exactly where she was. She was experiencing real peace and joy. Curiosity kept her alive.

Being in touch with her soul showed her how to grasp her inner kindness even when nobody was looking. She discovered how important it is not to look for rewards; kindness is the reward in and of itself. She admitted to not needing the applause anymore for what she could accomplish physically. In the end; it was just Ailill... in God's waiting room.

At this moment by giving up all her medications, and taking responsibility for her own choices, Ailill took the lead in her own story. Against all advice, she could accept her truth or deny her inner calling not to ingest poison and let nature take its course. She was afraid it won't be a very inspirational ending because this heroine fell short of the callings, broke down on her path and ran away from many trials. Giving up all her power is where she found strength. She realized she would never be as deeply connected to her soul as she aspired to be. Expectations, yearnings, and desires were not there to fuel her search through medical intervention anymore. She became willing to be vulnerable and to believe in herself despite appearances because she was all she could handle. She couldn't escape her future tripping and quit rehearing her fears of facing her failures when she met Saint Peter at the gate. Navigating the dark night of the soul she learned to integrate her disasters and not get stuck in blaming herself. Ailill graduated from being a child of God to sense that she was a grownup now. The lesson she learned in her words was; "If I live my destiny as infirmed as I am, it is still perfectly imperfect. I will never have to try to live someone else's dream ever again. Only I can bring my inner light to every corner of my inner self. It was never a contest; I am the mistakes, disasters, losses, and missteps that shaped my life. I was shown that suffering without pain is a waste if I don't choose life."

Ailill learned she could give herself new challenges despite how she felt. Her husband, John celebrates with her when she can walk down the hall. It is as big as the accomplishment of completing the climb of Mt. Everest. Her heart rate, blood pressure, dizziness gives her the adrenalin rush of a marathon runner just walking down the hall. Turning scars into stars is finding joy in the unimaginable. Death is just a new beginning; living in a sick aging body didn't have to diminish her spirit. The satisfaction of the simple victories of getting out of bed and taking a shower could now be called the victory that it was.

Slowly she was giving herself back to herself. She just had to reevaluate who she is and realize she was not who people said she was. She knew it was time to finish her journey by pulling off her masks and quit working so hard at being good and looking good. Ailill still struggled with having the experience of bats in her stomach. She claimed that no one would understand what most of her family members would get out of her soulful wonderings? I was proving to them that she had been in hiding. She was still afraid of their judgment and withdrawing their love. Because she did not want to acknowledge her eccentricity of being the "Woo Woo" grandmother, or that she did live in another dimension, she didn't talk about it because she felt like she was a true alien in their eyes. Maybe it's true but Ailill was born this way. Besides, she was laughing at herself thinking maybe her "Hide and Seek" game was only with her private self and everyone else could see her clearly. Have you also noticed that God does have an inconceivable sense of humor? I love the little saying: "We make plans and God Laughs."

Her mother, Mary O'Sullivan was truly a powerful physic. She would recall her life in Atlantis. As a child, Ailill was confused by her insight. For instance, one night she had a girlfriend over for dinner who witnessed conversations her family regularly had and thought nothing of. Her middle sister, Reagan asked her mother that night if she remembered when she about six years old, at the Payette River, wearing a pink poker dot dress with black patent leather shoes and lacy socks. Reagan explained; "I remember coming to you and telling you that you were going to be my mother and you ignored me." That is when Ailill became aware in a big way of how strange her family was. Her girlfriend shared her experience with everyone at school and the ridicule, name-calling, and bullying were on. Ailill's humiliation and embracement have had a lot to do with her hiding over the years. Her mother could bio-locate and describe places she had never been to with exact precision. Her mother, Mary shared her frustration with her four children that they didn't astral travel, telling all four of them how easy it was. Her mother would share the experiences her brother, Maddox O'Sullivan who was engaged in service while being in Vietnam and throughout his twenty-eight years of being a Marine. It was a challenge having a mom that knew everything long before you did. Her aunt, Annikki who was one of the sisters who came from Finland, was a popular physic connection for the Boise police department long before it was considered a viable resource. The detectives would bring her articles of clothing or other evidence they had collected and her aunt would hold it and direct them to the missing child or criminal. Another thing she remembered that day as if it was yesterday was that night after dinner she asked Ailill to go out and lay on the lawn with her to look at the stars. As they laid there she told her every soul in the universe is a sparkling star in infinity and we get to see just a little of it from here. Aunt Annikki asked her: "Do you ever wonder where your light is shining?" Ailill intuitively now sees the lights of all my loved ones who have died, even now, in shining stars.

Ailill's acceptance of her inherited insight has been that of a gift and a curse. When she would forget that others don't see what she does, it has caused her turmoil over the years. For instance, some of her greatest fumbles have been when she was facilitating group therapy. She used the technique called the Johari Window which helped people to categorize conscious and subconscious areas of their life. A client would be in the center of the group and she would say things like: "Tell us about the lady in the red bathrobe with the grey topknot." The incident was a burglary her client committed while high on drugs in which the lady died of a heart attack. Because it was later declared natural causes, he wasn't caught and no one knew about the incident. The crime was exposed in front of thirty people who were in the group. Her clinical supervisor was forced to call in the police and he was charged with involuntary manslaughter. In another group, Ailill asked the client why she was seeing a gray 1957 Chevy that appeared to be stuck in the sand. This client had injected his heroine and then he had prepared and given a shot to his buddy sitting next to him. He died of an overdose. Again, no one knew this but him. You can imagine the frustration of her director and colleagues. When she was working inside the prisons the warden called her into his office. He shared his frustration with her openly because he said the inmate's fought against having her as their therapist because she could read their minds. He accused her of being physic; Ailill assured him she was not physic because she couldn't call on it anytime she wanted. Ailill explained that the images would only appear when it served someone else. She tried to explain that it was not of her it just would come through her. As she was walking out of his office it occurred to her to ask him to allow her to continue to wear the jacket of mind reader and physic because it made my job so much easier. Court-ordered clients are masters at lip service and manipulation. They would lie even when it would be easier, to tell the truth. When they believed they were exposed it cut through lots of behaviors and BS that would delay their recovery. She had never liked being labeled physic but during this time of her life, she had fun with allowing others to see her that way.

Another funny story is when Ailill and her husband, John Star were visiting her sisters Quinn and Reagan in Florida. Reagan shared a past life dream while they were eating lunch. Her engineer, scientific, right-brained husband was flabbergasted and astounded because they always talked about their dreams. Reagan was reciting every detail of a dream Ailill had months before. The dream took place sometime in the 17th century in France and Ailill's & Regan's parents wherein the dream as Ailill's children. Cobblestone streets, horse-drawn carriages, and her sexy sister, Reagan were standing under a gas lamp were the exact details of the dream Ailill had. To this day when her husband and Ailill discuss their dreams, he tells her to call her sister to see if they are having the same dream. The mysteries of past life recall versus collective consciousness remains a mystery to most of us as to the origin of where do serendipity and providence begin and leave off.

Her little sister, Quinn on the other hand openly admits how both of her sisters scare her because she believes they are truly spooky. While doing an angel card reading for Reagan their little sister, Quinn would run out the door every time. Ailill and Regan loved sharing with all their ultra-conservative family members. They would tease them about fairies, divas', elementals, leprechauns, and angels. Ailill and Reagan are both artists and find lots of inspiration in their insights into the unseen. As I write Ailill's story it has occurred to me how she did invite making fun of her eccentricity, but it is truly a real experience for the spooky sisters. Her husband doesn't know how to explain Ailill when called upon to describe her because she disagrees with being called physic. Ailill admits she channels spirit and she knows she doesn't have a physic bone in my body. She is comfortable with the word channel because she believes everyone channels; what do you think prayer is? One day while they were in their office doing Auric and Chakra Imagining (I will explain more about this wonderful science in another chapter) and Reading Ailill was out to lunch with a friend

94

when a potential new client came in saying she had heard about Ailill. Her husband said he told her she wasn't physic; he said he did tell her that Ailill could tell her what her children had for breakfast and the clothes they were wearing when they left for school. Ailill couldn't believe he said that. The new client made an appointment and Ailill was nervous about what this lady was expecting because she never got her information that way.

Ailill eventually loved being unique and different. That statement has taken her years in acknowledging and accepting. From the time she was a young girl; she would see Arc Angel Michael and have long discussions with him. She couldn't tell anyone, but when people wanted to know how she knew what she knew, Ailill was missing an explanation. For over forty years Melchizedek has come to Ailill in her dreams and shared his guidance. He didn't identify himself until the last few years. Her husband researched him because he is a biblical scholar and one more time personally witnessed her universal connections in real-time. Genesis introduces *Melchizedek* – a "priest of God most High," as he blesses Abram.

Psalm 110: (KJV) is talking about Jesus,
"you are a priest forever, in the order of *Melchizedek*.'". I loved her dreams of a man who was here 4000 years ago.

The Faceless Maiden

Another gift of proof in how Ailill discovered we are forever all connected happened one day in her office. She gave out a scream as she stumbled on another coincidence. Coincidence continues to be God saying "Hi" to her. But, it still surprises her every time. Her husband goes back into her office to see what her squeals were about and there was a painting on her computer screen that she had painted from her imagination. The original painting was over 3000 years old and she had painted every detail without ever seeing it. The fun mystery with this piece of art is that she called it the "Faceless Maiden". Ailill explained that she tried to paint the face of the maiden over a hundred times and it just wouldn't work. She finally gave up and left her anonymous and unidentified. This is what she wrote at one of her art shows where the theme was Every Painting Tells a Story: "This painting was inspired by a dream which symbolically showed the first wishing well in Ireland and the Stonehenge of England. Christians believe the swan to be a symbol of grace and purity, it symbolizes the Virgin Mary. Ancient Romans believed that the swan was a symbol of a happy death. In

96

Celtic folklore, swans were a symbol of love and purity, their music was considered magical. The Faceless Maiden is the imagination of each of us. The direction, intention, and imagination of life are what allow our self-portraits, which are like none other in the whole world. This is why the maiden insisted on being without a face."

In another chapter, I will share with you how spirit paints through her art. Ailill's art is the voice of her soul.

Chapter 10

If It Is Important to You – You Will Find a Way

"You can't reach for anything new if your hands are full of yesterday's junk."
~Louise Smith~

"Either I will find a way or I will make one."
~Philip Sidney ~

Hear the Heart of Me:

Our hearts can speak; each of us has a personal language. Ailill's diary was dramatic and vivid and she wrote about what happened in her life story. It was a privately written saga to herself about herself. It's the past that tells us who we are. That is when she discovered it had all happened inside of her. She realized how her parents and grandparents existence was dependant on those isolated incidents of heroism, tragedy, pain and many incidents like that. Ailill knew it was remarkable to still be alive, mobile and breathing, after losing the number of family members she has lost – her sibling, her parents, her husband, two daughters, life long friends; they're all gone, her only relatives now are those she had herself produced and their offspring. Never could she have imagined letting go of the tiniest bit of her family. Ailill wrote to herself;" I guess that's just how resilient I was forced to become. All her life so many things happened to threatened her life and yet she was alive, telling herself stories of her yore.

Ailill realized how her existence was also dependant on each single incident happening one at a time. If anything would have happened to her then she wouldn't be here writing this piece.

Ailill wrote; my existence is dependant on my parents, on my grandparents on their parents and so on. How everything present now depends on so many things that have happened before. This dependence can be taken back to the formation of the Earth, the Solar system and the universe; everything out of nothing. She wrote about the thoughts that passed through her one after another spontaneously. At the end of the realization, everything culminated to form a single thought.

I'm Lucky.

I'm lucky to be present now, at this moment, alive.

I'm lucky to be a part of a chain. The long chain of events that resulted in my being.

I'm lucky when I wonder what would happen if a single link in this never-ending chain would have gone missing.

And I'm lucky to know I'm lucky.

It gives me Goosebumps thinking that everything I experienced or I came across were not random incidents but results of actions done long before I existed. Making me feel the events and incidents happening are especially orchestrated for me.

But it makes me sad seeing people ruining their lives. They run, fight, kill, steal all over petty things that add no meaning to their life.

It's like the two chicken stories I heard sometime back.

Once there were two chickens, arguing which food they find tastier. One liked cracked corn while the other mealworms. Both were lost in their conversation, to which the butcher was listening with a smirk on his face.

Truth is, both of the chickens were completely missing the point that nothing is tastier than this **life**. The life they have taken for granted which is going to end pretty soon.

To be present now is the greatest gift anyone can have. We are indeed very lucky to experience this life every passing moment.

Everyday countless die yet we are here to feel the earth with our bare feet, smell the air after rain, embrace our beloved. If this is not being lucky then I don't know what is.

We let our problems, desires and chores take control over us while we miss the truth which is the cornerstone of every experience we have. It is because we **exist** that we experience all this stuff.

The simple reason that we are here now, should be enough to bring a smile to our faces.

Ailill knew we are nothing compared to the infinitely vast Cosmos. But out of all the odds, we are here. And it makes us special, a star made from stardust. In examining her own life during this long illness she found that every one of us is a kind and extraordinary soul.

She wondered if she took more than she gave in life. She had made choices to get herself what she wanted; not realizing how much it might have hurt everyone else. She thought to get where she wanted to be and having everything she needed, she had to run faster, work harder and push and push until she crashed and burned. She never sought a life that leaves behind destruction, pain and sadness.

Ailill would work seventy hours a week with prisoners, inmates and patients. She worked at juvenile halls and group homes. She spent most of her time with twelve-step groups, sponsors and lost souls. Brianna, her beautiful daughter, once said to her: "Mom I am a single mother of five children and I guess I would have your attention if I was a crack addict on welfare." She heard it and yet she didn't know how to take off her superwoman suit or how to get off her runaway train.

Now, at this late stage of her life, saying she was sorry didn't make up for a lifetime of being absent. She only hoped they would see her through the eyes and heart of this old crone which she had now become. Looking back she recognized that her pearl of wisdom was more about her lack of wisdom.

Ailill hoped that people would understand the glorious blessings that each and every one of us is endowed with in our lifetimes would be seen, not through accomplishments and running harder but by being present in the moment. She has reached another rite of passage in this last chapter of her life. She learned that with all her hunger for knowledge, college education and reading hundreds of books; she now recognizes how much she doesn't know. I think that is true intelligence. Studies now verify that the most successful happy people in the world have a high P.Q. (personality quotient) not a high I.Q.

I witnessed the freedom, joy and personal delight she found in releasing her old worn-out patterns. She frantically wanted to share her feelings of love as she didn't know when her expiration date would be. All she knew for sure was that she had less time in front of her than behind her.

She didn't have to know everything or be right anymore. She accepted that she doesn't think and believe like most people. She knew that includes some of her family. You will hear stories about this eccentric grandmother and its crazy how that used to hurt her feelings but today she accepts who she is. Just a crazy, wacky grandmother who has so much love in her heart she hardly knows what to do with it, thus she chooses to shower the whole world with every once she can muster.

Some of O'Sullivan's generational traits strongly support striving to be too perfect, achieving success, comparing and competing which ends up being total insanity. They learned that they needed to look good on the outside while they abandoned their true selves because being human; we are all always only striving to be recognized and loved.

Most of the O'Sullivan's have labeled each other as workaholics. Nobody fell far from the apple tree. Our education, teachers, religion, and the messages of our western civilization also program us to be perfect and compare and compete.

Ailill was sad about seeing how all of us are marching faster and faster to the negative critics that live in our heads. Her adult children, now in their fifty's have just recently shared with her that they hated what they called her psychobabble, but they now realize while they did hear her they are only now beginning to understand..Ailill rejoiced at how successful, loving, committed, productive citizens and sensitive people she was related to. She saw all of them as divinely perfect and wished that they could see themselves through her eyes; the majesty of who each and every one of them is and how proud she is of them all. She confesses to not knowing how to express the pride that swells within her heart.

She had laughingly told people that God doesn't have grandchildren or favorites. But guess what, she does! Ailill taught me that the task of life is to face our sacred moments, listen to and follow our intuition but only what's true for you. Not how the world tells you to be. Only you know what God created you to be. For the first time in her life, she understood the concept of just being and not pushing to just be a human-doing.

As she aged she came to know without a shadow of a doubt that we are already the person we are looking for. We are just human. What we are looking for we are looking with. Ailill wrote in her diary; "I didn't create my eyes, my ears, my family members or even who I would love. God never makes mistakes. I am an individualized creature of the Highest." Think about it; you and I are God's idea. We witness the beautiful essence of each other. It just doesn't get better than that for each one of us no matter what!

There are no mistakes in God's world. That is not an empty aphorism or proverb, it is a fact you can take to the bank.

Ailill wrote about the long conversations she had with her daughters while they each in turn laid in bed fighting to survive forth stage cancer. One of the main topics each daughter talked about often was death and how they saw or felt about themselves at this stage in their lives.

Kaitlyn Norse lived in California and Ann Bailey lived in Florida but they shared the exact same statement; "I wish I had been a better person." Ailill was challenged by this as she saw each of them as practically perfect in every way. Now that she was, for all

102

intents and purposes beginning to understand, learning via her own life review she realized she was often too nice and too accommodating to so many other people in her life which may have led her to experience many compromising situations.

Ailill reflected on what it was that her first counselor tried to teach her after she first got sober which was how to accept her own humanism. Life may not repeat itself but it definitely has the same rhythm. She was 40 years old at the time and now her daughters in their early forties were facing the same challenges but from their death bed.

Ailill was motivated to re-read her journal written 1981 to refresh her memory of how she learned to accept her humanism. She shared her personal entrees with each daughter.

"When you acknowledge your humanness, you understand that you won't be perfect; that perfect is impossible – instead of hating yourself for the standards you didn't reach, or beating yourself up over what you didn't achieve, you smile with pride at where you are and push yourself to begin again. You acknowledge that you are a person, and give yourself space to start over and to heal. When you accept your beautiful, messy humanness you realize the physical is only a tiny portion of one's identity. When you look in the mirror, you don't see your flaws first; instead you see a soul, a person, an entity and rather than placing so much value on the outside physicality of yourself you search deeper. Even when you fail, even when you mess up, even when you don't feel beautiful inside, you realize that these good and bad moments of your life are teaching you who you are. Instead of chiding yourself for not always doing the right thing, you begin to understand that your experience – positive and negative – is building you. And you celebrate this: your imperfect, beautiful humanness. Sometimes the growth is in the journey

Ailill shared with her daughters that she knew it was her missteps that intensified her need for God's guidance and when she became so sick and tired of being sick and tired was when she surrendered to life on life's terms. Easier said then done!

Ailill had many names for the debate committee that lived in her head: Critical parent voices, the naysayer, Ego, Monkey Mind, and Shitty Committee. When all of the board members of the Shitty Committee gather then we need to recognize that we are each of us in really bad company. Her daughter Kaitlyn referred to this as her own private war zone.

Now she believes in an all-knowing, ever-present universal loving creator she calls God, whose multi-universe is perfectly orchestrated by His law, in other words, everything is in divine order. Newton's third law of motion validates that for her. It states that every action has an equal and opposite reaction. This means that forces always act in pairs. Action and reaction forces are equal and opposite, but they are not balanced forces because they act differently on different objects so they don't cancel out each other.

She used to pray and tell God what she needed as if He was like a Cosmic Santa Claus. Now she knows and has proven to herself that the power of attraction is the gift God gave us to create our heaven or hell right here on earth. When she pleaded from the point of view of excessive neediness she was given exactly what she prayed for, more neediness.

Ailill told me that she did not realize she had so much personal accountability. She wanted a merciful God to do all the work and just send His blessings. Now she has realized that the God of her understanding honors the image she was created in and honors her choices in ways she never understood before.

We truly are the co-creators of our destiny through our powerful gift of choice. In other words, we are our creator's vessels. God didn't do it to me or for you; the universal life force only honors and blesses us as the recipient of the perfect law of cause and effect. No favoritism, no judgments, no blame, no punishments and no rewards. Ailill knew that she did reap what she sowed. One of the greatest gifts her daughter, Kaitlyn gave her from her death bed was her excitement when she exclaimed; "Mom, I promise you it isn't just good drugs, I saw Jesus, Andrew, and other loving spirits. You are so right in everything you have said. We are all **Perfectly Imperfect.**"

Ailill has wanted to make bumper stickers in memory of her daughter's epiphany. She witnessed numerous times how when we are ready to make our transition back to the eternal heavenly home that we have one foot in our earthly body and another foot in angel land. It is a dimension that vibrates with energy that is present at all times. She hopes each of you will meet your spirit team and discover that the Holy Spirit never takes coffee breaks.

She knew and hoped when she got to the other side it would be her who gets to whisper in her loved ones ears. She knew how to communicate with her spirit team and always knew when departed loved ones were with her. She said; "To feel them now is like being closer to them than when they were here in their physical bodies. I am sure when I am on the other side I will share every moment with my Soul family, so be aware of your sacred connections, see every butterfly, every hummingbird and feather at your feet."

Everything that has happened to you or me has value. Nothing is right or wrong. It is the thinking that makes it so. Ailill's son gave her a tiny little book, As a Man Thinketh, when he was first baptized many years ago. She still treasures the message of how not to judge anything.

(Mat 7:1 KJV) Judge not, that ye be not judged. For with what judgment ye judge, ye shall be judged: and with what measure ye mete, it shall be measured to you again.

"Do not judge or you too will be judged. For in the same way you judge others, you will be judged, and with the measure you use, it will be measured to you".

Today we hear it called the power of attraction. Today we recognize the power of changing our thinking and how that can change our lives almost instantly. It is our thinking that shows up in our lives. Our thoughts are things. It's true that when we dare to change our consciousness, the whole world around us changes.

Look at the wonderful blessing and life Ailill had because she discovered God's calling in her life. She was only eighteen months sober when she was asked to share at a speaker's meeting. A man gave her his card and asked her to come to his office that following

Monday for an interview. At the time, she was a financial representative at a local savings and loan. A single mom of three teenagers, building a log house and show barn for her Arabian horses, attending family counseling at an adolescent treatment center, attending AA meetings for herself, personal counseling sessions and learning how to live life without numbing out.

As she sat in his office she chatted with educated counselors, (MFW's), probation officers and social workers. "What in the world, was I doing here" she wondered? After he hired her and offered to send her to Boise State University for her certification, she asked him why he hired her and not the other already educated prospects. He said, "It was when I asked you why alcoholics and addicts use and abuse at the cost of losing everything in their life?" She remembers there was a long silence before she responded with; "Is that a trick question?" They really can't do anything else because it is even more powerful than our will." He said, "Your experience is something education could never give you." At that moment God used all her experiences, failures, character weaknesses, alcoholism and total brokenness for the power of good.

There was to be a lot more crisis, chaos, missteps and wrong turns on her path, all of which were derived from poor choices she would make which turned out to be bad for her future, however as she learned and began to make changes everything else changed. Even today when hard, hurtful and painful times happen she knows she is back in school for some soul growth and the outcome always has real value and purpose. Ailill learned that no matter the appearances or how harsh or difficult the lessons, things that show up in her life will have a value she may not understand at that moment, but she can trust that life happens for the Highest and best good of every single soul in the Universe. We are all God's children doing the best we can to find our way, even when negative life forces seem to be relentless. The true universal energy is the God Source, and energy has no boundaries.

Without a doubt, some of the darkest times she and her three teenage children had to endure were the two years after her first divorce. It was a judge who sent her daughters to drug and alcohol treatment. The runaway rebellion of her teenagers was intense. They lost their parents and they lost their way of life. They had only known skiing in Lake Arrowhead, sailing regattas at the Yacht Club, with their sailboats right at the front door. They had to leave their friends, and their mother was in the latter stages of her alcoholism. Her recovery had many jumpstarts because she kept trying to sober up for her children. She learned that if you try to do it for anyone else it just doesn't work. It might sound selfish but it isn't really. It is Self-ish. You have to do it for your Self first and foremost so you can be there for them.

After their initial no contact; a ten-day blackout at the treatment center, she went to visit her baby girls. They came running down the hall saying;" Mommy, Mommy we are alcoholic addicts." Ailill was livid, she ran into the director's office screaming: "What in the hell do you people do here, brainwash babies?" She had never heard the word alcoholic before, though that was her childhood experience. An alcoholic in her understanding was a bag lady that lived under the bridge and an addict was someone who had track marks running up and down both arms. Her beautiful precious fourteen and fifteen-year-old daughters did not come anywhere close to her understanding of what addiction was.

Doctor Crusade, the director of the center calmly asked her to sit down and he said; "I have been waiting for you because we need to talk about your drinking." Ailill's justifying minimizing and rationalizing alcoholic mind immediately went into high gear denial. She thought, "My drinking problem? Look at everything I have to deal with and you want to talk about my drinking?" In the next 60 days after attending family counseling and education classes, she remembers being so surprised that everyone was talking about her life and they didn't even know her. It was from this place that her daughter, Kaitlyn was sent to the adolescent center for her anorexia and bulimia. Her oldest daughter, Brianna came back home and she became Ailill's total caregiver with responsibilities that no fifteen years old should ever have to shoulder. Ailill was suicidal and in a deep depression. Her son ran away. He went back to his father who provided him with an apartment and a car.

The O'Sullivan clan has the gift of humor even during their tragedies. When Ailill was building the log house she had a ranch hand. This man, Tom Horn endured so much. Ailill and her three children laughingly recall when he invited the four of them out to dinner and he came in his pickup. Her son was quick to share with Tom that the last time he had been in a car to go to dinner was with his father who was in a Rolls Royce.

This man had asked Ailill to marry him every day for four years and every day she would say no. One day when Ailill came out of a drunken blackout, to her surprise, she was married to her second husband. Her son had already run away and her two daughters were very angry and upset that she didn't invite them to her wedding. What they didn't understand was that she couldn't invite them because she wasn't even consciously there. They still talk about it today; what that poor man had to endure. Her kids let Tom know regularly they would never shovel horse chit, (their words), and they were above anything he had to say and battered him because he was just an Idaho cowboy.

Today they acknowledge the care and dedication he gave all of them in spite of their ridicule. Ailill divorced him after five years because of the all encompassing complication of him being her number one drinking buddy. After recovery, they grew apart. He continued to support her long after the divorce by helping her move her furniture to California after she sold the horse ranch. He even occasionally came to visit her where she lived for several years alone on her sailboat.

Every cloud in each chapter of her life has always had a silver lining. She was instrumental in helping Tom Horn reunite with his three estranged adult children. Her children were no longer with her but his two sons and daughter still continue to communicate with her to this day.

At this juncture, she realized that her grandchildren may someday read about their parents in their teenage years. I believe they will begin to understand what incredible survivors and awesome role models their parents have become. All three adult children have become heroes in their own right. Ailill claims that they grew up in spite of her. All three of them raised themselves from a very early age. She acknowledged that they are the parents that she was unable to be. They are successful in their own lives both monetarily and spiritually.

At the time of this writing, there are ten grandchildren ranging in age from twelve to thirty-two. Someday her two great-grandchildren can read this and honor their grandparents and the lengths they had to go through themselves and how they were able to rise above their lonely challenges with such grace and dignity.

Ailill filled her diary with praises for her adult children.I am heartfelt and struggling here because even as she puts it, there just aren't enough words in the English language to properly express how proud she is of her whole family. She prayed that all of the cousins; nurture, protect, honor and love each other and she hopes they all realize it just doesn't get better than family connections. Don't wait until old age to see that love and family are what you take with you. Love can never die. Love is not an attribute of God but Love Is God.

Ailill's diary referred to her being an absentee mother, daughter, sister, and grandmother but the gifts that have come from her families sacrifice are magnanimous. For over Thirty-Three years she has had the privilege and honor of giving to others what she could never give to her own family. Her calling has been very intense but also very gratifying. She has been blessed with the privilege of sharing her family's pains and challenges; their experiences, their battles and victories with thousands of others.

I do mean thousands, beginning at ARC in Oregon, moving on to developing Mental Health programs for women, having a private practice working with families and children, working for faith-based rehabilitation centers. She worked inside and outside the prisons in various states. She developed a program for young mothers on welfare. She worked five years in youth homes with the adolescence that were abandoned and broken due to their parent's addictions. Ailill even worked in group homes with adolescent boys who were sex offenders. She has worked with hardcore men incarcerated from fifteen to twenty-five years.

Her son mentioned to her a few years back how she has spent a lifetime with criminals, street people, and the lost souls. He didn't understand at the time but she told him that she never met any of the people he described because she only saw the light of God in every soul she ever met.

109

For over forty years, Ailill said this silent prayer with everyone she met, every group therapy and anytime she was asked to speak at a meeting, at a college, or one-on-one sessions; "Dear God, may the Christ in me speak to the Christ in you, and please get Ailill out of the way". She explained to her son, "That might be what they did, but that is not who they are".

That insight has truly been a gift from God. She sometimes wished she had inverted eyeballs so she could see herself as clearly as she saw everyone else. She only had perfect vision when she saw others. Ailill wrote about what magnanimous looks like. Her closest loved ones are the precious people that through their forfeiture of a mom and grandmother and the agony associated with all that, they have allowed all of that healing to happen. How can she ever begin to say Thank You!

Over the years Ailill has received hundreds of letters and e-mails from past clients expressing gratitude for the life they have today because her family lived their story. The experience, strength and hope of the O'Sullivan clan will live on through hundreds of people because they lived the story of taking their scars and turning them into stars. Ailill's love for her family is overflowing with total gratitude for the blessings that each one of them brought to the healing table even if they were unaware of their own participation. She brags about coming from a large tribe of heroes and recognizes all her earth angels even if they don't know it.

Ailill shared with me what she learned from her family and how she shared it with so many others. Can you begin to imagine what a student of life she has become herself? Thousands of people did not know that they were her teachers; she would share with people as a therapist: "I can't fix you or change you because you already have all the answers inside of you. You already know the answers because there is only one expert on you and that is you. I can only encourage you while you learn to journey back to yourself. My prayer is that this becomes your reality".

Ailill wrote in her diary; "Our creator gave each of us a personal unique moral compass, emotions, feelings, and a brain. We have everything we need to discover our authentic self and communicate with God. I know that if God had a refrigerator your cute picture would be on it. We have been brainwashed into believing we are less than we are."

Even when she told herself "I don't know how to do this", she has learned there is something inside herself that does know. If it is important to you: You will find a way. Never give up on finding the way, your way. Do over's are allowed at every turn on our life's path. She loved do over's and sometimes she did it three times a day to get it right. She learned that even when one door shuts in our life, other doors are built to open. She has embraced the design for living through the 12 steps of Alcoholics Anonymous. Every morning she does the third step prayer which is turning her life and will over to the care of God. At night she does the seventh step prayer which consists of mentally rehearsing her day and questioning herself, where she might have been self-seeking, dishonest or unkind?

There are two gifts in this prayer. First, you don't have to carry the burden of your missteps or mistakes into the next day. You empty daily the garbage bag you used to carry on your shoulders that was overflowing in guilt and shame. Secondly, you get to choose if you're going to learn from your mistakes, and remember it's not about persons, places or things because the only thing you have power over is cleaning up your side of the street. We all get to right the wrongs wherever possible.

Ailill says, "In a small way before I leave this world I get to put into words some of the wrongs I have made. It has been exhausting to try to be something I'm not. All I can do today is live life under the principle of trying to be a better person every day. I like to believe that every kindness is a little bit of love that I have left behind."

Ailill puts these little sayings on sticky notes and places them on her bathroom mirror or refrigerator because as she puts it, she has an amazing forgetter. She used them to help her remember to stay out of the driver's seat, not live in her negative mind set, and to offer everything up to God.

- Learn to listen because nothing is wasted.
- Thoughts become things.
- Live in gratitude.
- My soul is what connects me to all beings.
- When I live in God, I live in love.
- My soul can be my watcher on the wall.
- Dear <u>Ailill</u>

.....I won't be needing your help today

... Thanks Anyway Love God.

Insert your name on your sticky note and write to yourself as a reminder of who really is in charge. These little reminders helped Ailill to remember to surrender to God. Fake it until you make it and prove to yourself the power of faith.

- Break my silence and walk out of shame. (This statement inspired her to write this book.)
- Being vulnerable is finding honest reference and dignity for yourself.
- You are the change you want to see in the world.
- I am no better than anyone else and nobody is better than me.
- Give pieces of yourself via empathy, not sympathy.
- What people need and love most is appreciation.
- We sin when our love is out of balance.

She has kept her gratitude diary for over thirty years. The joy expressed within those pages is amazing. Ailill considers it to be the number one spiritual discipline that works every time. Rereading her gratitude list daily she discovered she can't even begin to want anything because she already has everything.

Chapter 11

A Picture is Worth a Thousand Words

"The drawing shows me at a glance what would be spread over ten pages in a book."
Ivan Turgenev, *Fathers and Sons (1862)*

Ailill was fifty-eight years old before she picked up the paintbrush and decided to walk through an age-old fear; "I'll never be good enough." Her sister and mother are/were amazing talented artists and she was in awe of their talent all her life. She knew there would never be a way she could do what they did as well as they did because she thought that she just didn't have the talent. She remembers painting her first painting in her living room; because she was in the process of remodeling she could let the paint fall and splatter without worry. She remembers her husband, John coming home from work that day and she immediately went into a Happy Dance, jumping up and down and squealing with delight. "Look at this, can you believe that came out of me?"

From that moment on, she surrendered her inhabitations. Her spirit and soul took over. It wasn't about being good enough; it was deeper than that, deeper even than her ego's voice.

Her still small voice is God, intuition, spirit, guiding light and inner promptings.

Since she believed in a God that is the All, Ailill accepted the fact that there was nothing unsafe about pursuing God. She had jumped off the cliff before and was free-falling into the unknown. God had shown up every time. She decided to take whatever risks she needed to take to experience the blessing of getting closer to the promptings of her soul. She became willing to have God turn her life upside down, reshape her values and redirect her energy. Rather than trying to stay inside her comfort zones, she was open to saying yes. Whenever her higher-self called she listened and followed with anticipation for new adventures. She did not expect this encounter to inspire such awe and wonder in such a magnanimous way. She called herself an aspiring Grandma Moses, and to date, she has created more than 200 art pieces, including painted tiles, lamps, and murals. She has painted floors and walls all over her home. Her paintings have been shown in many art galleries up and down the Central Coast of California. True to Ailill's compulsive personality she spent thousands of hours studying art, reading books, watching YouTube, taking classes, and watching recorded CDs of hundreds of other artists. She became self-taught, learning and perfecting her own style. Others describe her as a diversified eclectic artist. She has two online galleries, Red Bubble and Fine Art America. This is one of her introduction statements.

Painting the Beauty of Heaven and Earth through my Vision

By Ailill O'Sullivan

As long as I can remember I could sense color around people and I am sensitive to the feel and essence of the energy that surrounds people, places and things. It is how I discovered my intuitive abilities and began my professional life as a counselor over 30 years ago. Artists abound in my family and we have thrived in our mutual creativity. Studying obsessively physiology, philosophies and human emotions has become a large part of my creative stew. I use the word obsessively because my finished work so rarely equals the initial impulse or conception thus compelling me to start over and try again. It is always my love for life that stirs up complex feelings, leaving me aching to express new ideas. This is the reason why my art is so divergent in style, mediums, and compositions.

115

The inspiration to better understand the mysteries that lie beyond normal perception is what led her to art and the study of auras. Every plant, animal, and human is surrounded by an electromagnetic energy field that emanates from our bodies. While few can see it, it can be felt by all as the "vibes" that someone gives off and how others experience them. Energy is expressed in vibrant colors. She is thrilled that technology and science can now allow us to view our colorful essence through bio-feedback. The universe is full of inspiration, that is what everyone can see but it takes courage to pick up a paint brush and attempt to illustrate thoughts, visions and this beautiful universe into magnificent art. Ailill is always looking to create meaning in her work. Art is the medium for the bigger message. Her artwork ranges from dream-like, abstract pieces and realism. She intends that her paintings inspire others. Beauty is in the eyes of the beholder. She intends to show the passion and allow the viewers of her art to resonate with their own beauty, innermost self, and creativity. Ailill is so grateful for the blessing and expresses her joy to have the privilege of bringing beauty into the world.

Ailill had a dream that mother earth came to talk to her. She thought about it for days and days and wondered why such an unusual topic would surface now. She was motivated by what she calls an epiphany. How mysterious that a message like this would enter her subconscious. An epiphany for her is usually a sudden manifestation or perception of the essential nature or meaning of something. For instance, her first impression and introduction to Gaia came to her during a Reiki treatment with her Reiki Master. She never knew that some called Mother Earth Gaia until this encounter. Our earth does have the essence of a living thing. She has often wondered how different our society might be if we had listened to our Native American ancestors. What a different world we would have if we had learned from them hundreds of years ago.

Ailill's art is a visual of her life's journey. It truly depicts for her a powerful way of what she writes in her journal and diary. She particularly loved her painting titled 'New World.' The inspiration for this painting wasn't totally clear at the time she painted it. She just let it flow, which is her creative style and why she calls her work a visual meditation. She had completed this painting shortly after Christmas. As many of you know her youngest daughter,

Kaitlyn made her transition on January 18, 2013. She gave her youngest daughter a white statue of an angel for Christmas. Kaitlyn asked her to keep it and paint it for her. Kaitlyn said she wanted to be the Angel in a painting and she wanted to see herself with blonde hair. (I'm sure that was inspired by the fact that her daughter had lost her beautiful blonde hair during chemotherapy.)

Phoenix rising to a new world with the Angels represented to Ailill a world of holiness, free of pain, and suffering. The dove represented the Holy Spirit; Ailill continues to miss her daughter so much; she likes to think of her now on a journey of wonder and joy. Sometimes just looking at this painting would give her a little bit of comfort and remind her of a special angel who stays very close to her.

Ailill painted a large seascape that was inspired by her last trip to Maui Hawaii two months before her terminal diagnosis. She and her husband snorkeled with the turtles for days. She reminisced how she would dive down with them and then when one would surface they would face each other. They did this for hours at a time. One day while playing in the waves in front of their hotel the large turtles showed up in the surf and swam with them. They stopped on a deserted beach and a giant turtle was taking a nap in the sun. The giant turtles followed her everywhere she and her husband went that week in Maui. She wrote in her diary about the magical mystical serene feeling she felt that only these beautiful ancient creatures could create.

Ailill has been drawn to the water since she was a little girl, swimming in oceans, rivers, lakes, and streams. Living on her sailboat for 5-years she would call pods of Dolphins and follow them around laughing and playing with them for hours on end while out at sea. Her fascination with the sea, fish, seascapes, and sailboats has been the inspiration for much of her artwork. The added pleasure of painting these particular subjects required her to study them in their habitat, their mannerisms, and every facet of their colors and personalities.

I would love to share her entire gallery with you but that is impossible in this venue. I can share some of the descriptions of her sea life gallery, which led to some comical lifetime memories. One description was of sea horses down deep in an ocean canyon

117

looking at each other. Their expressions inspired the title, "I See You." This whimsical fantasy composition includes those sea horses which have become one of her favorite subjects to paint.

Ailill described the sea horse as an amazing wonder. The dark canyon walls with the light reflection add to the mystery of this undersea landscape. The patterns, colors, and style literally created itself. The expression of the sea horses looking at each other in such a quizzical way added to the fantasy and humor of this painting.

'The Mural Painted on the Back of her Home'

Ailill and her husband John traveled to Florida on numerous occasions to visit her stepdaughter. A highlight was the beautiful murals painted by the artist named Wyland. He was known for his Wyland Walls. That's when she became inspired and decided that she wanted to paint an Ailill Wall. Of course, another contributing factor was that snorkeling all over the world, her number one favorite sport. This is the mural she painted in her backyard. It is 40 feet long and 8 feet high. She painted water, waves, and sand on the patio floor which added a different dimension.

The funny part of this project was when the neighborhood children would climb the fence to see what she was doing. They would ask her, "Why was painting big fish on her house?" She would respond by telling them, "I am just a crazy artist." She became known in the neighborhood as the crazy artist who paints fish on her house. Notice the grey-haired man wearing a snorkel and mask looking down at the mermaid. That is her husband John who often comments he didn't know he married a mermaid until she introduced him to the beautiful world of undersea life.

Ailill enjoyed the whimsical interpretations of her sea life characters. She loves "Nemo". Clownfish get their names because of their stripes and their bouncing movements which make them look like clowns. All clownfish are born males. When a female dies, the most dominant clownfish then changes into a female. Snorkeling with them in the Caribbean was truly an astonishing journey even though Ailill was in her late 60's.

In her painting titled Down Deep, the fish's expressions reminded her of the Seven Dwarfs; Sleepy, Grumpy and Bashful.

She was excited about this newspaper article because many of her family and friends haven't seen it. This was the beginning of an amazing journey.

Inside the artists' studio
Is life art? In this home, yes it is.

NORA K. WALLACE, NEWS-PRESS STAFF WRITER
There's no mistaking Ailill's workspace in her home. In addition to colorful Painted caterpillars and a large canvas depicting an ostrich, there's an oversized artist's palette on the floor, spots marked with splotches of yellow, orange, purple and red paint.

Mrs. O'Sullivan couldn't be happier about being a part of the tour.

"People are so interested in where you create," she said. "That's part of the wonder, what space you create in. We're all different."

Her own space is a small alcove, separated from her bedroom by a hanging curtain.

"That's what fun about a studio is," she explained. "You get to break all the rules."

119

Her entire house is her canvas, the bedroom wall painted with faux brick and a castle scene; the bathroom of her husband John, painted in a tropical image with toucans; and her kitchen, with a birdhouse mural on the wall and painted white picket fence at the floorboards.

"I haven't found a niche yet," said the 62-year-old Mrs. O'Sullivan, who moved to the Central Coast about four years ago. "I'm an aspiring Grandma Moses. I always want to try something different."

She calls her pieces "Visual Meditations" and didn't start painting until she retired three years ago.

For 22 years, she worked as a drug and alcohol counselor. In the three years since leaving her job, she's done little more than "sleep and create, sleep and create."
She's churned out 80 pieces.

She has shown in places in numerous locations throughout the valley.

"My art is like a free gift," she said with a boisterous laugh. "I've paid my dues. I have such a passion for it ... This isn't working. This is so much fun."

***

Looking back on her life's journey has been an astounding realization and an affirmation that she did do life on that runaway train. Since the time that article was written, she has flunked retirement three times and embarked on three new businesses. The blessings of being In God's waiting room have proven to reveal the wondrous fully packed life that is now only in slow motion. If her wheels hadn't fallen off she would have missed the scenery and joy of seeing herself through new eyes. She would have missed the boat if she wasn't willing to become a rookie in all areas of life. Stepping out of her comfort zone and not believing she was too old has allowed her to transcend disappointments she had harbored for years.

The visual illumination of her experiences which she calls, her still small voice, her intuition, her personal communications with spirit and her spirit team have all allowed her to acknowledge that God speaks to us awakening the third eye and the connection we all share. The title of her painting "Guardians" depicts her spirit team. It is an expression of the unseen that works through her but is not of her. This is the voice of spirit and her muse; The same voice she hears in her meditations, while she journals, prays or paints..

"Art enables us to find ourselves and lose ourselves at the same time."
Thomas Merton

A close friend and fellow artist described her own work as having conversations with her canvas. Another ah-ha moment was when Ailill realized that is exactly what she did also. She had never actually labeled it that way for herself before. She reviewed her descriptions of her art and I want to share with you some of her conversations. I found many interpretations through her paintings of flowers, oceans, butterflies, the colors of the Caribbean, abstract expressions, animals, birds, and angels.

Ailill shared with me a funny story about her then five-year-old grandson who came to visit one day. He said; "Grandma why do you paint so many flowers?" She told him; "I see God's face in every flower I paint." Her grandson then proceeded to put his face very close to the flowers on her patio for almost three minutes. When he looked up he told her; "I can't see God's face in them."

Ailill intends for her art to provoke the viewer to find their own interpretation and become conscious of what moves them. The abstract painting that she titled Bird's Eye View speaks to her in a very unconventional way. In her imagination, she wondered what their world really looks like through branches of trees and behind flowers when flying overhead. She visualized a surreal universe in stunning patterns through their eyes.

This whimsical painting she titled, Heck of a Hat, was a festive cheerful experience where she challenged herself using her mind's eye. She created whimsical images that resonated with her bliss. She laughingly loved her anorexic arms. So tiny compared to the stack of cleavage on top don't you think? As she reminisced over this painting she commented that; "Maybe I wasn't meant to be an artist. When I sell one of my paintings I get a feeling of deep sadness like a piece of me just walked out the door. Maybe that is because I put my heart and soul into each piece. I am sure that my work comes from the soulful food that inspires me and it's where my intuition becomes visible."

Ailill's art is a kaleidoscope of inspiration. She sees it in everyday objects, riding down the street, or sitting in her backyard when the moon is shining. She wrote in her diary that she thinks she has a monkey mind when it comes to art. She continually has about 6 compositions and visions running around in her head at any given time.

Her passion meets her vision with intense energy and bright colors. Her version may be overdone in reality but not in her imagination. Ailill believes every human on earth is an artist. Our perceptions are one of a kind. We are the author of what we see, how we choose to see it, the life that we choose to live, and how we choose to express ourselves.

The gift of being an artist is allowing it literally to create itself, much like life on life's terms. We're the ones that see the various angles, shapes, and miscellaneous details through our own unique one of a kind understanding. Her husband John often remarked; "That he didn't notice his world until we married Ailill who taught him to see the world through an artists' eyes." It could be because he does the photographs for most of her inspirations and she has taken him outside and shown him how to look at just the shadows for hours at a time, studying only shadows for eight hours at a time. Did I mention her compulsive addictive personality? If a little bit is good, allot is better in every area of her life or yours.

The newspaper article that follows is only a summary of her tribute to her youngest daughter, Kaitlyn Norse and her battle with cancer. Her daughter had a statue of a dragon because she had a dream that the dragon was going to eat her cancer. When Ailill and Kaitlyn would go to chemotherapy treatments in San Francisco, she would take the dragon in her purse as it symbolized healing so she included the dragon in this painting.

The girl skiing down the mountain is her youngest daughter, who was given a wish, comes true and skied down the powdered slopes in Valdez Alaska. She did this with fourth stage melanoma in her lungs. Her tumor was the size of a nine-month-old fetus. The large tumors had metastasized to skin cancer on her back. Pink roses were her favorite flower. The ocean represented her passion for water skiing and water sports. She was featured on CNN for skiing to Catalina Island and back. She also participated in the International Women's Ski race in Australia. Kaitlyn, two grandchildren and her husband, Will held a prayerful light for Kaitlyn's diligence as she battled with her cancer. Arch Angel Michael was who she saw in her dreams throughout her thirty-six-month fight. Her daughter was truly blessed with the warrior spirit. Metastasized melanoma is the worst cancer you can have because there is still no known cure. She was given three to six months to live at the time of her diagnosis. She endured all kinds of medical trials so that science might learn more about this type of cancer.

This picture says more than a thousand words because of the volumes of experiences throughout the last three years of her life. During medical trials, her daughter was tested with IL-2 where they took her to a coma state to be tested. Her bravery throughout the many experiments was nothing short of heroic.

One day when mother and daughter showed up for chemotherapy treatments Ailill was invited into a staff meeting concerning her daughter's case. She was surprised at the large number of scientists, doctors, lab technicians and other medical staff present in that meeting. Kaitlyn's oncologist said, "In his experience, it was not just her daughter who had the diagnosis of later stage metastasized melanoma but the entire family now suffered from this terminal disease". Ailill admits she didn't understand his reasoning at the time, but she does now. He was wrong about Ailill being able to withstand what ensued next. Seeing the large tumor on the screen and all of the so called professional conversations about her daughter's illness was so cold and unfeeling that she stood up and emotionally erupted, interrupting their discussions. "My daughter is so much more than a specimen in your Petri dish, her name is Kaitlyn Norse." she left the room hysterical. Later her oncologist hugged her explaining why everyone had to emotionally detach because she was only forty years old with children who were only three and four years old.

"The Path to Healing - A Hero's Journey"

This painting is a complement to Kaitlyn Norse, Ailill O'Sullivan's youngest daughters' heroic journey through her fight with cancer, which ended Jan. 18, 2013.

Ailill was the artist of the month for February at a local gallery. A visual journal in paintings was the theme of the show.

"Every work of art tells its own story," said Ailill. "The main thing is to be moved, to love, to hope, to tremble, to live. Art doesn't have to be pretty. It has to be meaningful. I am interested in art as a means of living a life; not as a means of making a living. Art attracts us only by what it reveals about our most secret self."

Ailill's original education and experience began as a commercial and residential designer for 17 years, working exclusively for a large restaurant chain in which she and her x-husband were partners.

Changing her course of study she spent the next 21 years working as a counselor and teacher.

"Life experience has given me the insights and fervor of my artwork today. Every Work of Art Tells its Own Story. This is my theme because life has taught me how to illuminate the beauty of ordinary scenes," said Ailill. "I passionately create from a very different vantage point than exact realism in that; it is the emotion and song of art that means the most to me. Art is a literacy of the heart. Art is when you hear a knocking from your soul, and you answer."

Ailill was given international advertising rights by Hay House for her piece titled Winter Reflections. The interesting fact concerning this contract is that it not only applies to her life but also that of her heirs. Ailill's artwork is currently being shown throughout numerous galleries. She is also an active member of several art associations.

"I am really excited about my show," said Ailill. I have included fun short stories on my labels. It should be fun. I am known as the Peacock Lady because I have painted many compositions featuring these fascinating birds."

Chapter 12

Creating a New Treasure Map for the
Future

"With age, gone are the forever's of youth. Gone is the willingness to procrastinate, delay, to play the waiting game. Now each day is a treasure beyond compare . . . because there are so few such diadems   left."
~ Joe L. Wheeler ~

(I admit it – I Flunked Retirement)

There are many theories regarding how things in life should be during those golden years. Ailill went into high gear in an attempt to disprove the experts on the theories of aging. She eventually reached a point when she stopped lying about her age and started bragging about it. She hoped to stay young forever but she noticed she started labeling herself as 'Old Crone and Grandma Moses'. She has since realized she will be emotionally immature forever because it's more fun than acting like a grown up. Ailill has a close girlfriend who ends her letter and e-mails with this quote:

"Life should NOT be a journey to the grave with the intention of arriving safely, not in an attractive and well-preserved body, but rather to skid in sideways, chocolate in one hand, martini in the other, body thoroughly used up, totally worn out and screaming "WOO-HOO what a ride!"

Something strange happened when she turned sixty-five. She likened it to the energy rush you get before the new baby is born or the pig-out one does before you start a new diet. The saying use it before you lose began to grow on her. She began to think she had to hurry because her internal odometer may be getting close to its expiration date. She started and ran three new businesses. She was the spiritual editor for a local newspaper called Vision. Good News You Can Use. She opened her own art gallery where she combined her Aura & Chakra imagining business. She became a Reiki Master and taught classes at a local College.

The following article written by Joe Payne of a newspaper was especially comical because of his title he chose for the article. Joe was a very tall, robust man, with a deep voice and strong manly demeanor. His title' Pretty in Pink' would make anybody who knew him laugh out loud. His insides just didn't match his outsides.

Capture your color: Ailill O'Sullivan shares her art, aura and chakra video photography skills at Aura Therapies Gallery
BY JOE PAYNE

Pretty In Pink

As soon as I place my fingers on the contact points of a biofeedback reader attached to a computer and monitor at Aura Therapies Gallery in Old Orcutt, colors begin to dance across a still image of my face, captured moments before. Reds, oranges, and violets take turns on the screen, accompanied by text that lists the various traits connected to each color. The overall effect is then recorded by Aura Therapies Gallery owner Ailill O'Sullivan, who excitedly reacts to the information the technology and software provide.

"Whoa, look at those, look at your colors!" she says. "Look at how big your aura is! Oh, my dear, you have tremendous power!" Whatever power Alhart is referring to, it can't be the power to quickly understand auras. Much of our time in my aura and chakra video photography session is spent on O'Sullivan explaining what an aura is.

"There is an electromagnetic energy field around all people and animals," she says. "We are body, mind, and spirit, and now, with science, we can see and feel the spirit." Words like "spirit" and "energy" tend to raise skeptics' hackles in most scientific discussions, but O'Sullivan uses her technology to help people relate to themselves. A retired therapist and counselor, she often surprises people—this reporter included—with knowledge about their personality minutes after an initial aura reading.

"Auras don't lie; they can't because it's pure energy," she says. "It's so much fun. People always say, 'How did you know that?'"

Each person's aura is a result of the health and balance of his or her chakras, O'Sullivan explains. A session with her includes a reading of your aura, the size of your chakras, and the balance between your chakras. Depending on your aura colors and chakra balance, you may land anywhere on a diverse spectrum.

127

"Everybody is very, very individual," she says. "No two people are alike."

Along with your results, information pertaining to each aspect of your aura and chakra reading is included in a 24-page packet for your reference. Each chakra is connected to different aspects of personality, emotion, and spirit, O'Sullivan explains and helps determine your aura color and balance. The entire package is a kind of psycho-spiritual Myers-Briggs test.

"It's very exciting because for the first time our technology is allowing us to look at this energy," she says. "No one is saying we know exactly what it is, because it's beyond our physical intelligence."

Though O'Sullivan worked as a therapist and counselor, she stresses that her aura readings are meant for personal understanding of emotional and spiritual well-being, something that's helped her understand herself. It's also helped her realize her gift and love for painting, with many of her works hanging in her gallery for sale.

"All of my painting is guided visualization," she says. "I meditate in color."

O'Sullivan hopes to help people who are open to the idea of auras and chakras for personal understanding and development. Her gallery also includes a lending library full of books relating to auras, chakras, dreams, and spirituality. She's not afraid to ask deep questions—and hopes others will help her seek answers—but she also has plenty of information to share about biofeedback, auras, and energy.

"You are the expert on you," she says. "What do you feel? Who are you? How do you resonate? What color are you?"

THE BEGINNING OF THE LOMPOC VISION

With the initial advice that good news just doesn't sell, Jordan took a gamble and has since become our cities premier dealer of "Good News You Can Use." Arriving here from London, England in

1964, Jordan took every opportunity to immerse himself in the local culture.

When the Visions' Founder isn't out and about the town doling out stacks of fresh newspaper, he's acting as his own administrative assistant, funding source, sales department, design team, manager and CEO.

Some said that it was impossible to start a paper without a financial backer". Recognizing the naysayers as potential for growth, Jordan accepted the challenge; worked hard to sell ads and three weeks later printed the very first Lompoc Vision in 2003. His takeaway: "Don't believe the box people will try to put you in, you are limitless!!

Enclosed are some of Ailill's favorite articles:
Lompoc Vision
April 2009

Ailill O'Sullivan

From Outward Appearance to Inner Substance

Thank you every one of you who have taken the time to write and call to share your inspirations, personal experiencing and thoughts concerning my articles. I continue to be in awe and gratitude that a monthly newspaper is now sharing only "Good News You Can Use". I am in the process of expanding my education and working on a degree from the American Institute of Holistic Theology. I am excited about validating my years of successful experience in being a hypnotherapist and dream interruption therapist through the study of Carl Jung philosophy with archetypical symbols and understanding the subconscious. This Spiritual Journey series I have published here is for each of you to experience and enjoy as a tool I have used for over twenty years to allow each of us to access our true inner self, authentic self, window to the subconscious or individual spiritual essence. As you can see, we can use vast terminology which all leads to the same place. The purpose is to come to understand and appreciate the individual beauty of you. As each of us learns just how unique and wonderful each precious person is, we will out picture that energy to everyone in our world. This is the root solution of any dilemma we may be facing. Simply put we will then come to know it really "Isn't good or bad, right or wrong it's just the thinking that makes it so.

These one-line journal statements are worded so they will expose your passion, opposing viewpoints, curiosity, possibly anger, and humor. Use these statements as a tool to articulate what your world looks like through the filters of your unique expression. Feelings are the language of the heart and soul, so pay particular attention to the statements that trigger an emotional response. Have fun and continue to e-mail me your experiences and "AH-HA MOMENTS".

Contempt prior to investigation enslaves us in everlasting ignorance.

Expectations, the source of *all* unhappiness, tend to live in an illusionary bubble of fantasy No one knows who or what God is, your love, belief, and faith allows for a living God.
We cannot begin to fathom the awesomeness of God in our mortal minds.

We need to stop acting like children of a lesser God. What if God commanded nothing, what if the commandments were a covenant, of a loving God?

Compete and compare, let's loose the ugly habit of society's conditioning!
Where does a thought go after you think it? The brain alone can't think so who's doing the talking?
Will the still small voice everyone is talking about speak up, please? The universe is impartial, make good choices and good things happen, and make bad choices bad things happen
It rains on the just and the unjust.
Garbage in – garbage out
A person who learns to laugh at themselves is amused most of the time. God doesn't make junk and he didn't start with you. When you hate yourself or claim that you are not good enough it's like a slap in God's face
This is pride in reverse, who are we to slander the creator's work?
If I think I can, I will; If I think I can't, I won't. What you think of me is none of my business; it's what I think of me that count.
Practice the presence of God, omnipresent, omniscient, and

omnipotent. Maybe God is the indivisible air between all objects and inside our bodies. Who knows? Seeking God is like looking for something that could never be lost.

What you are looking for, you are looking with, and we did not create the eyes that see.

Surrender to win; it is the opposite of all conditioning in life.

Acceptance does not mean you have to like it.

Unconditional regard for all is the ultimate goal.

If you are constantly told you look like a duck and talk like a duck, you will soon believe you are a duck.

Love dissolves fear.

God IS love; Not the attribute of a higher deity

Get out of the driver's seat; claim a higher new manager for you, some call this reborn. Act as if everything is exactly the way it is supposed to be

There are no mistakes in God's world

We are encouraged to be against ourselves, call off the war; it's so much more fun than confusion and indecision

I am sorry that the people that hurt you didn't know how to give you love.

Let me love you until you learn to love yourself

All of us are coming together in a renewed community of healing, sharing and talking about the real issues. It is an exciting time of renewal and coming together Continue to Grow and Glow and as we practice learning gratitude together, love and life can only expand to the next highest best level we have ever experienced before, in spite of adversity and challenge.

We will know intuitively that it is because of the adversity and challenges that our joy grows and grows.

Lompoc Vision
May 2009

Ailill O'Sullivan

Consider what Spirituality – Is or is not:

Hello everyone. I am enjoying the feedback and experiences everyone is sharing with me concerning their new awareness and new ways of understanding the importance of the power of our individual beliefs and faith. **Good News You Can Use** is the foundation and goal of aspiring to a new vision and The Vision

Newspaper is the founder and edited by Victor Jordon is just that. Many of you have shared that some of the insights I have shared now live taped to your refrigerators, dashboards of your cars and/or on your bathroom mirrors to remind yourself of the power of positive thinking and the power of attraction. Thank you for taking the time to share your experience and feelings of how many of you are not willing to buy into the negative energy of the personal challenges facing many of us today. As the one-liner for easy remembrance seems to be so popular, I have continued to include them in this series. This series is truly Good News You Can Use. When we feel and hear the good news that resonates deep inside of us it can be called our individual spirit recognition or spirituality. I have taken the liberty to insert a clarification of an often confused buzz word called spirituality which is only your truth. Consider how and why you can resonate only with YOUR truth:

- Spirituality is not a religion, church affiliation, or even belief systems. It has to do with our spirit. Our *Spirit Individually* meaning Spirituality
- Spirituality has to do with the quality of our relationships with whomever or whatever is most important in our life
- Whatever or whoever is "Most Important". It defines the main focus of our spirituality
- Spirituality is closely related to values, priorities, goals, and preoccupations. It has to do with whatever is at the center of our life
- A Spiritual issue could be anything that makes our relationships with others more or less loving and caring
- Spirituality has to do with the things which are the "Loves" of our life. We will find our hearts invested heavily in the spiritual areas of our life
- Spiritual relationships evolve from how a person has experienced life or how he or she has come to deal with life situations
- Spirituality emphasizes the need for a Higher Power
- Spirituality is a life force which provides the energy for growth that enables us to move beyond ourselves and experience a passion for a commitment to a cause greater than ourselves
- Spirituality can be a simple set of guidelines

- Values are simply the rules that one lives by; the development of the value system becomes a major aspect of spirituality
- Spirituality is the development of an attitude of grateful living
- Spirituality becomes the love of our lives when our heart is invested
- The first quest for spiritual (individual spirit) human fulfillment was possibly for camaraderie and togetherness. This is a basic human need and a simple desire to be happy.
- As we change our spiritual focus, we will necessarily develop a different lifestyle because what is important to us has changed
- Renewed spirituality will lead to restored sanity
- The principals of spirituality are so simple that most of us miss them
- That is probably why we can use the **Good News** of a one-liner truth statement: Remember the guidelines: Throw away what doesn't fit and embrace your "AH HA's" as your truth. The joy and power of being "Your Authentic Self" is then realized.
- We are more alike than different; we all have the same needs and wants.
- Unhappiness comes from converting our wants to needs.
- Love the journey, even the detours.
- You never have and never will do anything except exactly what you wanted to be doing
- When you own that truth about yourself, all power will be restored.
- Who said you had to be better, most and different? By what authority?
- Question all thoughts that sabotage your acceptance and peace of mind.
- After living in crisis and chaos, harmony and peace may look and feel boring
- Being sick and crazy works. No one will ever expect anything from you
- Permit yourself to trust even after you've been had by a master manipulator
- Break the chain of sins visiting us for generation upon generation

- Stop blaming, and making up excuses, take responsibility for your own beliefs and actions
- We make it up as we go along, so why not rewrite our story
- Being left alone with yourself when you are depressed or in despair; you are in really bad company.
- Let peace begin with me.
- Co-dependency is chaining a soul.
- Your trials and tribulations are your greatest gifts, they are the real teachers.
- Take off your super-human suit, no more running harder or going faster just to feel normal.
- Celebrate your triumphs; don't focus on your blemishes and short-comings.
- The crisis and pain in our universe is newsworthy because it is truly the exception. We tend to forget that!
- We all honor each other's choices even if they choose to be a criminal. Let us begin to remember that is what they do and not to be confused with who they are.
- Financial security is not a check in the mail, but gratitude for what is available.
- Take inventory and feel rich
- Gurus in drag are not necessarily the problem; we sometimes don't see them as gifts.
- Keep it simple stupid..........kiss
- Behavior modification isn't about skill but attitude
- If today is the beginning of the rest of your life, release it and start it over as many times as you need to.
- Do it all for free and for fun.
- Don't let your left hand know what your right hand is doing
- The universe is benevolent, the rest is a lie
- No one can hurt you unless you give them permission
- Don't surrender your power
- Ego...........Easing God Out
- Did you know that 90% of our planet believes in God?
- Who said we are going to hell?
- There is no "I" in teamwork.
- Defenses keep out the very thing you need the most, a connection with another soul
- If everyone is truly one, put on a new pair of glasses and see everyone else as you.

Laughing Dolphins

The Lompoc Vision
August 2008
Ailill O'Sullivan

THE ROLE OF LAUGHTER

Lesson's of laughter that I teach is what I would like to share with you. I have given this poem to many clients who had just forgotten or never been told how special each of us is. It goes like this. (Put this in your pocket for your rainy days).

The psychology I teach is only you.
  Your truth; you are the expert of you.
  Your authentic self is tried and true;
  It is the only healer because it is the total of you.
  The mental and emotional process is uniquely your traits,
  Attitudes and thoughts are your creations.

The growth of the soul is what you came here to do. We are advanced in mind and body but the spirit needs to catch up too, so overlooked and unnoticed. Be your truth, call off the lie, God didn't make junk and he didn't start with you. The creator of all doesn't have favorites, no grandchildren you see; he loves all of you and me. You didn't create you, so when will we stop rejecting God's best stuff? Today you can claim to the world that the game is off. You are your Highest Best Good, just as your creator intended. Try this exercise for yourself and see how often you can laugh at yourself. Laughter truly is the best medicine. Mentally, emotionally, physically and spiritually it touches every human component. Have fun with this. What you are looking for you are looking with. Everything you will ever need may be found within your own body, heart, and spirit. Your most difficult task is to believe in yourself. Using these practices, exercises, prayers and self-help methods, perhaps you will learn to reawaken the trust in your wisdom, courage, and creativity.

We do this work in the name of love – love for ourselves, love for our family and friends, love for all the children of the earth who have suffered. As the capacity to love expands within you, your love, kindness, and generosity become available for others – and the family of earth is in desperate need of your love, your care, and your participation in the growth and healing of us all.

Chapter 13

Natural Solutions – What is Reiki

"Energy work is priceless. It makes every day extraordinary and Transforms the mundane to the holy."

Silvia Hartmann

Experience the Power of Unseen Energy

Ailill became acquainted with Reiki when she met a Reiki Master, Haruto Sora who had an office in the same building as her gallery. Ailill watched Haruto's clients coming and going and she witnessed what seemed like miraculous results as they progressed through their treatment over a course of just a few weeks. She was struck by the fact that Haruto's clients all seemed to exhibit an overall healthy glow in addition to major healing. Ailill was especially intrigued because she sees and read auras. Ailill made an appointment with her and from that moment on she was a believer. She realized that this could augment what she was doing with her aura readings. So, as one thing lead to another and Haruto Sora became her Sensei (master/teacher). Ailill worked and studied her way through Reiki One and Reiki Two eventually becoming certified as a Reiki Master. A simple explanation is that a Reiki practitioner is a channel for healing energy. This universal life force continues to act on the body long after the actual treatment. Ailill documented volumes about her experiences with her clients, some of whom are my friends and family. I am personally amused when someone who is curious about Reiki uses terms like hocus-pocus or likens it to faith healing due to not understanding this pure and simple ancient healing technique.

Reiki is a specific technique of energy healing which was founded by Mikao Usui who was born in Japan in 1865. Master, (Sensei), Usui discovered this technique in 1922 and eventually built a school to bring this knowledge to many students. Rei- (pronounced ray) refers to spiritual wisdom and Ki- (pronounced key) refers to life energy. Basically practitioners work with a person's vital life force energy which is the same energy that animates every living thing. In China it is called Chi, in Sanskit it is Prana and it is also sometimes referred to as the Bio-Field Energy. It might seem difficult to explain to the layman but the concept is really quite simple.

The practitioner places their hands in a series of positions slightly above the body. It works by activating stress reduction and deep relaxation allowing the body to balance thereby promoting healing. Reiki is for everyone and it is especially helpful for those who are seeking pain relief.

Energy healing has been practiced for thousands of years and works naturally on many levels; emotional, physical, mental and spiritual. The Reiki student must be certified to practice by achieving three different levels or degrees of certification. Students who have been certified for levels one and two may practice their healing art gaining experience thereby honing their expertise. By the time the student is certified for level three they become a Reiki Master and at this point they may pass on their wisdom and skills by initiating and certifying other students by attuning them to the Reiki energy. This powerful healing technique can be learned by anyone. Reiki is not a religion or a cult. Ailill had prior knowledge that energy is tangible and cannot be created or destroyed. Becoming a Reiki Master for Ailill was a complement to her Aura & Chakra Photography and imaging business. Working with energy medicine for Ailill which was once labeled eccentric and Woo-Woo was now a visual scientific method of proof that she could openly share with other. Her excitement and joy was unimaginable with her new discovery. It works and is generally beneficial for the client whether they believe in it or not. Energy healing has been around and practiced for thousands of years..... Reiki itself was only discovered in 1922.

One of Ailill's clients who is a devote Catholic asked if it was ethical for her to experience it. Ailill explained to her that her personal experience was like being bathed in the healing light of the Holy Spirit. She decided to see for herself and as it turned out she had a profound spiritual experience. Ever since that day she has been one of Ailill's best advocates telling people what it feels like to have a bath in your insides from the Holy Spirit. Some of her clients have experiences like meeting their Guardian Angel, seeing loved ones who have passed over, immediate relief of tension and some see vibrant rainbows. Others have reported experiencing intense emotional shifts and cleansing during the treatment process. Everyone's experience is unique because every one of us is unique. Ailill loves hearing what transpires for each person before and after their treatment. She claims she could write a book on their experiences alone.

Another client shared what she wrote in her personal journal after her first experience. "Once I arrived, I was greeted by this very "down-to-earth" woman. I was honestly "expecting" an old gypsy woman to appear, whatever that means. She greeted me with such an open heart and very deep spiritual eyes. At this time in my life, I was feeling very numb to the relationships I had, the direction I was heading, and I had no clue what the human energy system consisted of.

My stepfather had just passed away -- whom I was very close with -- my boyfriend and I were in a riff, I didn't want to be working as a waitress forever and I had a great amount of anxiety over what I should be pursuing in life.

As we entered the room, she explained to me that I would be fully clothed and her hands would hover a few inches from my body or lightly touch the skin. I felt confused yet open to experiencing something new. I remember within the first ten minutes feeling a total numbness throughout my entire body. I peeked my eyes open just to make sure all my limbs were still intact. She explained in the beginning that many of her clients experience numbness, tingling, or an "out of body" feeling. I was not expecting to feel this sensation so precisely.

I don't think I had ever given myself even an hour of the day to feel myself and my energy before. I was just learning how to meditate through my yoga teacher training and understanding the power of our thoughts, but this was the first time I was in a room with someone who truly recognized my soul and all the energy points within my body.

I had many visions throughout the session of me traveling through exotic countries, meeting people I've never met before, and lastly, seeing my father clearly and feeling his presence. As her hands were placed on my heart tears flowed out of my eyes uncontrollably. I was not sobbing, but it was as if I was truly seen and felt for the first time. Once the session came to a close, I collected myself and was consciously led to bring my awareness back on earth into my body.

She shared with me the visions she saw, the sensations she felt, and as she was speaking, I had more emotional releases. It was unbelievable. How was it that this woman who knew nothing about me could see me so clearly?

I was slightly "freaked out", but more so, incredibly relieved, and felt I had just opened myself to a completely new chapter with fresh perspectives.

Reiki -- with this incredibly beautiful and talented practitioner -- changed my life. I remember driving home, rushing into my backyard to grab a pen and paper, laying out a blanket in the grass and writing down everything that happened, so I would never forget this experience. Reflecting back, now I see how that was one of the first awakening times of my life.

What is astounding is that with the biofeedback video photography, which essentially captures a snapshot of your aura, (your electromagnetic energy); Ailill can actually see proof of the change in a person's aura and chakras. The proof is in the pudding... Or, a picture is truly worth a thousand words.

When a person's energy is low it makes it difficult for the body to deal with stress and it can be susceptible to disease/illness. With Reiki it is possible to give your energy a boost helping your body to feel vital and assist your immune system to fight off illness and stress.

Our bodies and our brains are made up of mostly water. We are 90% water when we are born, about 70% water as an adult. This liquid must flow through our bodies at a smooth uninterrupted pace every second we are alive. Some people talk about "blocks of energy", I see it as similarity to a kinked hose. The water stops sometimes entirely if a hose is kinked tight enough. Swelling and stress are two ways of "kinking our arteries; allowing stress to accumulate in the arteries, sometime due to lack of exercise and insufficient water intake. Mental stress can also cause these blocks.

Reiki works when the person requesting the energy is focused on their own wellness and well-being. Sometime, just relieving stress for an hour or so with a Reiki session can work wonders on the human body. As the energy begins to flow through the body, the "kinks" are released reducing pain and stiffness in a potentially short time.

Ventura College now gives an Associate Arts degree in alternative healing modalities. Ailill and her husband are invited to be a guest speaker every semester because this is our future. The word Holistic is described as the comprehension of the parts of something as intimately interconnected and explicable only by reference to the whole. We are speaking about treating the body, mind, and soul. It is Ailill's background and knowledge of energy and how it manifests itself in our bodies that gave her the courage to stop all of her pharmaceutical medications after a year in bed.

The Five Reiki Principles
By Mikao Usui

Just for today, I will not anger.
Just for today, I will not worry.
Just for today, I will be grateful for all my blessings.
Just for today, I will work with honesty and integrity.
Just for today, I will be kind to all living things.

If you are drawn to Reiki, you should be aware that there is a reason. Ailill encourages everyone to explore this wonderful healing energy, treat yourself, enjoy a Reiki treatment or take a workshop. While she teaches courses in California, there are many wonderful Reiki practitioners all over the world. Be sure to find a teacher that resonates with you!

Ailill is confident that it is Reiki that has had such an impact on her life. When she was so ill she would go into her healing room and listen to ancient flute music and she would cleanse her chakras with the healing energy of Reiki and meditation. She attributes her being able to get out of bed to this graceful silent healer.

Ailill wrote about one of her experiencing while meditating one day last year. She heard that inner voice of hers telling her that she was about to begin the work she came here to do. She remembers suddenly opening her eyes and saying out loud; "Do you remember just how old I am?" She shared this experience with her husband, John who has a keen sense of retort and is always able to make her laugh. He said, "Be sure to take a long time doing it because I like having you around."

Chapter 14

Rainbows Exist in Everyone

"Dare to love yourself
as if you were a rainbow
with gold at both ends."
~ Author-Poet Aberjhani~

Get to know your vibes through Auras and Chakras.

Finally, science is proving what Ailill had known all her life. From the moment she discovered aura and chakra video photography which incorporates bio-feedback, she was all in. With bio-feedback, she could actually photograph a person's energy field. Chakras are the body's energy centers which, in turn, transmit your aura. Every one of us has a sixth sense in varying degrees. Most of us unconsciously recognize a person immediately, even before they speak or acknowledge us in any way. Sometimes for some people, who they are yells at them as soon as they enter a room. Have you ever heard the term, "I feel you?" Many people go through life unconsciously feeling their way around. We are picking up on the vibes of others or the vibes in a room. Actually, it is the individual energy field of a person, place or thing.

In Ailill's case, she is what some people refer to as a Sensitive, which just means that she is highly empathic. She feels the energy of a room full of people and she feels the energy of animals and plants. She has been doing that since she was very young. It's actually been a saving grace for her at times. Being sensitive to other people's energy is how she gets her information. She has used this ability unconsciously almost all my life as a survival tool. It is when she doesn't listen to it that causes the problem. She can sense who you are, what you're all about and know you. She understands what lies behind the mask people show the world.

Once Ailill discovered the wonderful bio-feedback system, she knew I was no longer going to be labeled as crazy or even psychic. She can now show people what she has always been able to see and feel in real-time using bio-feedback and photography. It's exciting for her when she can show someone their own aura for the first time and they discover the light body that has been with them probably into eternity. It is truly like flipping a switch to turn on a light and she never gets tired of that.

This has probably happened at least once in your life where you meet someone for the first time and you instantly like them or maybe you dislike them and you don't really know why or you get a bad feeling from a room that you just walked into. The explanation for that is that you are picking up the vibes around you or in other words, you are unconsciously feeling the energy around you. Your energy is mingling with other energies. We are literally like molecules constantly bumping into each other and then reacting to that energetic mingling.

When we talk about seeing auras we tend to think of people who see colors emanating from the body. Many believe that all children have this ability but lose it as they get older. Science is proving for us that we all have this capacity to feel and see the energy around us. Now we can all experience what that is like and ultimately what that means.

Seeing auras and learning about chakras seems to have become mainstream in the 1980s during what we lovingly refer to as the new age, however, ancient texts and traditions have imparted this knowledge to us sometimes handing down their secrets by word of mouth as in, shamans teaching shamans, healers teaching healers and so forth.

The human energy field is without a doubt the next frontier for western medicine. As scientists are exploring and doctors are beginning to understand, it just might be that most illnesses will be a thing of the past. Science has proven and charted the human aura as tangible energy so it is no longer a product of fantasy as some people would still have you believe. The human energy field, which is your aura, can absolutely show where illness exists in the body before it presents itself as symptoms on a physical level. There are also studies that prove that this energy is easily influenced, not only by the mind of a person in need of healing but also by educated practitioners who understand the ultimate possibilities.

144

Everything is energy. This is a simple concept of quantum physics. Concerning religion and spirituality, the movement of energy is a fundamental truth around which many traditions are based. Ancient healing practices such as Reiki, Acupuncture and even Yoga like Tai-Chi focus on the manipulation of energy to achieve well-being. We like to think of space as empty air and think of matter as solid but everything is energy vibrating at different frequencies. There is no such thing as empty space.

At the time she started her Aura and Chakra Imaging business she discovered that people had little or no understanding of what she was talking about and they often referred to it in the context of emotional healing or meditation practice. Many people still find the concept confusing. It seems the most confusing idea is what places this information might have in each of our lives. As it turns out, anyone can learn to work with these energies, not just the experts.

Each of our Chakras is an energy center unto itself that has a unique frequency and holds within it the knowledge of the inner workings of correlating systems in the body. Even a basic understanding of what we refer to as the 7 main chakras of the body can enhance your life in surprising ways.

Whether you are looking to heal a specific emotional/physical wound or working to improve your ability to manifest the highest best good in your life, which is recognized in certain circles as working with the Law of Attraction or just hoping to boost your overall well-being it pays to know more about these 7 chakras.

I invite you to explore each of the 7 chakras, their specific functions and corresponding colors. Ailill has always been able to physically see auras and she dreams and meditates in color so it isn't a great leap of faith for her to understand that about each of us. We are constantly radiating a rainbow of energy. She has studied and learned that each of these energy centers is what actually allows us to radiate our true essence at any given moment in time.

Chakras are constantly receiving and transmitting energy. There are many more than the usually referenced 7 chakras which are located along the spine from the top of your head to the tip of your tailbone. This means that each of us is a receiver and a transmitter. She believes that we are eternal spiritual beings on a human journey, so when she discovered a way to show people their own auras; AKA their spirit bodies, her enthusiasm went through the roof.

Energy is tangible; something we've discovered exits, and we are beginning to understand how to manipulate this force field that surrounds every human, plant and animal. Energy cannot be created or destroyed. It can and does change form but it can never be destroyed. We are constantly discovering new ways to harness and use it mostly for the betterment of the human race and also to expand our horizons by exploring the universe at large. The most exciting thing about all of this is that we are learning that we are that which we are exploring. Our bodies are a complete replica of our universe. Think about it this way; if we are ultimately nothing but energy, which cannot be destroyed, then the idea of eternity becomes an energetic reality.

Every book Ailill has read every class and experience she has had in her life had to happen for her so she could be here now to share this with you. Everything is in Divine Order. She has been fortunate and blessed to have taught many classes, conducted group/gestalt therapy and practiced hypnosis with her clients over the years, all of which has lead her to learn how to live her life understanding the true essence of the soul. It wasn't so much about learning as accepting what is. Each of us is a true light body and the discovery of our authentic self is an ever-evolving enigma. Sometimes we are more of an enigma to ourselves than to those around us.

Your Body's Seven Chakars

I Know

I See

I Speak

I Love

I Do

I Feel

I Am

This diagram shows the placement of the 7 chakras and highlights their corresponding function. Each Chakra is also connected to our endocrine systems. I am attempting to keep things fairly simple here. Visualizing and clearing these energy centers is the most effective self-healing practice she has personally discovered. Everyone can learn to do it, no special classes, no need for experts and as far as I know, it really doesn't conflict with any one's beliefs or faith.

Every color of the Chakras' demonstrates its own vibrational frequency. The root Chakra, which is located at the base of your spine or your tailbone, vibrates at a slower speed than the crown Chakra, which is located at the top of your head. These electrical frequencies vibrate outwardly from our bodies in seven different layers. The first layer, closest to the body, is known as our etheric body and the seventh layer out from that is connected to the celestial realm.

Our aura extends anywhere from 6 inches to 3 or more feet outwards from the body. It's usually described as being a denser energy nearer the body and gradually becoming lighter as it radiates out or further away from the body. With the help of bio-feedback we can glean information regarding the foundation of the electrical imprint of each person's energy field. It's like a fingerprint.

This information holds the key to learning about our possible destiny or gives us an inkling of our life's purpose. It can help us understand some of our strengths and weakness. Ailill has had the privilege of doing over 2000 readings in the past six years. Of course she has investigated her own aura as well and she usually presents as Indigo-Blue or totally White.

Cleansing and Clearing your chakras is easy and effective:

- Start with your root chakra and work upwards to your crown chakra.

- Visualize where it is located on your body.

- See the color in your minds eye and imagine the energy that is vibrating.

Repeat each affirmation 3 times out loud or silently to yourself.

Ailill does it daily – She thinks of it as an Energetic Spa Treatment that keeps working all day.

Energy medicine is unbelievably effective. Try it!

Root Chakra: Red

The root chakra is located at the base of our spine and corresponds to the color red. This chakra relates to our basic human instinct for survival, security and stability.

Affirmation: "I am a divine being of light, and I am peaceful, protected and secure."

Sacral Chakra: Orange

This chakra is located just below our navel in our lower abdominal region. The color of this chakra is a deep, saturated orange and relates to reproduction on a physical level, creativity and joy on an emotional level.

Affirmation: "I am radiant, beautiful and strong and enjoy a healthy passionate life."

Solar Plexus Chakra: Yellow

This chakra is located above our navel and directly in our stomach area and plays a vital role in our digestion. It glows bright yellow and pertains to issues of personal power and spiritual evolution.

Affirmation: "I am positively empowered and successful in all my ventures."

Heart Chakra: Green

The heart chakra is located in the center of your chest with vibrant green color. The Key issues related to the heart chakra are unconditional love, compassion and wellbeing.

Affirmation:" Love is the answer to everything in life, and I give and receive love effortlessly and unconditionally."

Throat Chakra: Blue

This chakra is centered in our throat and exudes a pale blue light. This is our ability to express and communicate clear thoughts and ideas. It relates to truth, independence and the ability to trust others.

Affirmation: "My thoughts are positive, and always express myself truthfully and clearly."

Third Eye Chakra: Indigo

The third eye chakra is positioned in the center of our foreheads between our eyebrows. It spins in a deep saturated blue, indigo and helps us to tap into inner guidance and divine vision. This chakra deals with developing intuitive clarity.

Affirmation: *"I am tuned into the divine universal wisdom and always understand the true meaning of life situations."*

Crown Chakra: White

The crown chakra is located at the top of our head and corresponds to violet and white color. The role this chakra is based in awakening consciousness and attaining enlightenment through integration of the self into one of universal intelligence.

Affirmation: *"I am complete and one with the divine energy."*

Chapter 15

Life's Path is About Seeing God in Everything

The Bible says He is... (KJV)
- Our shelter, refuge and hiding place (Psalm 91)
- The one who comforts us (2 Corinthians 1:3)
- Our healer (Psalm 103:3)
- The source of wisdom (James 1:5)
- And everything else we need!

Ailill had an office space in a cooperative community called Launch Pad. It was a new concept which provided conference rooms, on screen set up for power point presentations, podium, etc. The impression was think coffee shop with full kitchenette available all the time. Her co-workers asked her to present to a group called the Universal Church. She told them she had no idea of what that meant. They said she had a philosophy and belief in Pantheism. She had never heard the word before. How could she be something she had never heard of? They convinced her that even though she did not have a label for it, it was what she counseled, taught and in their opinion was the message she carried in her heart. They gave her a copy of the seven principles of Pantheism which states that they believed in the inherent worth and dignity of every person and encourage and support one another in their personal spiritual paths. Ailill took on the challenge even though she was nervous because it was a group of professionals from every walk of life and they wanted her to present on a topic she was unfamiliar with at the time. She spent several weeks researching and she did find that her heartfelt beliefs actually did correspond with the rules of Pantheism and she talked about how they applied to her life. This is what she shared with the group.

" All of you have personally and collectively demonstrated humility, awe, reverence, celebration and the search for deeper understanding which has invited me to a greater capacity of open-mindedness. I was not even aware that my overview of the mysteries and how I see the world had a title called Pantheism until Ean explained it to me. As a result, I researched everything I could find. In keeping with open-mindedness and mystery, I am presenting information in many instances from many schools of thought. I would like you to ask as I do "What If".

The divine universe is mysterious. Though we can understand the universe more adequately as scientific research proceeds, there will always be questions to which we will not yet have answers; and explanations of ultimate origins will always remain speculative. This is just another way of saying mystery.

Every spiritual tradition values the goal of peace over conflict, love over fear, understanding over judgment and good over evil. The reason we fail to achieve these long-range goals isn't a lack of wisdom. Libraries are stuffed with volumes of wise teachings. Rather, the failure is due to the short-range decisions we make between breakfast and dinner. This is what shapes our behavior, attitudes, beliefs, and even our brains.

This is a Higher Power that is not so much SUPER-natural as ULTRA-NATURAL It is a power, God or spirit with whom we must forge a new kind of relationship. Pantheism is the belief that everything is holy, often crudely called nature worship and associated with nature poets like Shelly and Coleridge.

See, the mountains kiss high heaven,
And the waves clasp one another;
No sister flower could be forgiven
If it disdained its brother;
And the sunlight clasps the earth,
And the moonbeams kiss the sea;--
What are all these kissing's worth,
If thou kiss not me?
Percy Shelly

Many of my paintings are included in this slide show as my artist bio states: My paintings reflect the romance and beauty of nature which inspires the soul. I am endlessly searching to show the tie between my subjects and my heart. The poetry of how I see the work is what allows my viewers to connect personally with my paintings.

Many World Pantheist Movement members belong to Unitarian Universalist congregations and some are UU ministers. They tell us that perhaps a third or a half of Unitarian Universalists are probably strongly sympathetic to Pantheism. The essence of Pantheism is a profound reverence for Nature and the wider Universe and an awed recognition of its power, beauty and mystery. Some Pantheists use the word God to describe these feelings, others prefer not to, to avoid ambiguity.

I can personally say it is an exciting time where spirituality, evolution, creation and science finally meet. Everything in the known universe is made of the same proton, neutrons and atoms. Even though we split the atom and are learning about quarks and how the anticipated behaviors and actions of these discoveries appear not to be random but self-actualized.

Spinoza considered it obvious that God and Universe have always been one and the same. The concept of the ultimate substance, God as Nature, amounts to what is becoming widely known as Pantheism and it generates a definition of God that was (and still is) very different from commonly accepted dogma. Three sayings: A pantheist would believe that the universe does have a personality. It wants to live and it creates life where life shouldn't be. It creates beauty where no one can see. It has ambition, taste, curiosity, and every other trait that a human could have and plenty more. Everyone is part of the whole. I believe that we are spiritual beings on a human journey. The mystery of what the eternal looks like is still a mystery.

The observer plays an active part in what he observes. We live in a participatory universe".

> The fountains mingle with the river,
> And the rivers with the ocean;
> The winds of heaven mix for ever
> With a sweet emotion;
> Nothing in the world is single;
> All things by a law divine
> In another's being mingled—
> Why not I with thine?
> Percy Shelley

Two of her favorite authors are Wayne Dryer and Carl Jung: A primary method for making sense of the world is by interpreting its symbols. We decode meaning through images and, often without realizing, we are swayed by the power of their attendant associations. A central proponent of this theory, iconic Swiss psychoanalyst Carl Gustaf Jung, made an academic case for it in the now, classic *Man and His Symbols*. The white swan in her painting is an archetypical symbol of having the air element it can mediate between the earthly realm and the heavenly world.

She showed a photograph taken from a NASA telescope showing the tiny blue dot of earth. That's here, that's home. That's us. On it everyone you love, everyone you know, everyone you ever heard of, every human being who ever was, lived out their lives. The total of our joy and suffering, thousands of confident religions, ideologies, and economic doctrines, every hunter and forager, every hero and coward, every creator and destroyer of civilization, every king and peasant, every young couple in love, every mother and father, hopeful child, inventor and explorer, every teacher of morals, every corrupt politician, every superstar, every supreme leader, every saint and sinner in the history of our species lived there; on a mote of dust suspended in a sunbeam.

Our attitude to nature has wavered during our history as a species, from reverence to dominance and back to reverence again according to the stages of our ecological relationship with nature.

Black Elk, of the Oglala Sioux, wrote: "Every dawn as it comes is a holy event, and every day is holy, for the light comes from your Father Wakan-Tanka; and also you must remember that the two-legged and all the other peoples who stand upon the earth are sacred and should be treated as such."

Today we are living through the greatest mass extinction of species since the end of the dinosaurs. Our grandchildren appear to be technological wizards and accomplished artists. Working with troubled youth for so many years she met many of these misunderstood, unsung courageous warriors.

Well, the Indians would tell this story to their children around the campfire. The story goes something like this:

Sometime in the future, the Indians said, the animals would begin to disappear. People would no longer see the wolf, or the bear, or the eagles. And, as the story goes; the giant trees would also disappear. People would fight with each other and not love each other. The beautiful rainbow in the sky would fade away, and people would not see the rainbow anymore. Well, children would come. And these children would love the animals, and they would bring back the animals. They would love trees, and they would bring back the giant trees. And these children would love other people and they would help people to live in peace with, each other. And these children would love the rainbow, and they would bring back the beautiful rainbow in the sky. For this reason, the Indians called these children the rainbow warriors.

Nancy Ann Tappe, a teacher and counselor, studied the human auric field, otherwise known as their electromagnetic field. The field surrounds every living thing. She even wrote a book about it called Understanding Your Life through Color. Through colors in the aura, she instituted a shockingly accurate and revealing way to psychologically profile a person using her new auric color method. The signs of an indigo child began even as early as in the 1950s with a few people. What she noticed was that 80 percent of the children born after 1980 had a new deep blue colored auric field. She called this new color indigo.

The terms Dyslexia, Hyper Active, and Hyper Kinetic may just be labels for energy beings we are just beginning to understand. Ailill's' son was labeled with all of these in school and she told him it was because he was so unique he was a star child. When he was ten years old he discovered it was something she made up to allow him to validate his uniqueness. He was so disappointed.

Is God everything, the physical world, including our bodies? This is a response of the observer. We create our bodies as we create the experience of our world. We now know why human beings keep pushing the envelope of what it means to be human. Our self-awareness extends beyond the cortex of our brain, which after all is merely a physical receiver for what consciousness wants to tell us. We are sub cortical creatures. We always have been, but like an infant that lives for today without a vision of adulthood, we are confined inside the present moment.

The present moment is a laboratory of possibilities. Infinite possibilities are embedded in higher consciousness. It's our destiny, enclosed in time and space, to unfold them one by one, to be amazed by what it means to be human, and then to move on to whatever lies ahead.

British scientist James Lovelock has proposed that the whole system of living creatures, rocks, oceans and atmosphere, combined with the process of evolution, has remained suitable for life over very long periods of time, even though the sun's output of heat has varied over time. Lovelock's name for this self-regulating system is Gaia. Gaia or Ge which is the Greek name is interpreted as the goddess of the earth. For many pagans and pantheists, Gaia has become almost a deity. Some think of her as a sort of super-organism with soul and awareness and purpose. Other pantheists would argue that Gaia is none other than the natural community of life and non-life on earth, once again, a "we" rather than a "she" or "it.

"The important thing is not to stop questioning; curiosity has its own reason for existing".
Albert Einstein

"Science without religion is lame, religion without science is blind". Albert Einstein

"The most beautiful experience we can have is the mysterious. It is the fundamental emotion that stands at the cradle of true art and true science". Albert Einstein

The awesome wonderful truth about this is that in a million years forward or backward there will never be an exact you or me. No two snowflakes or blades of grass are identical creations. Don't you find that this idea boggles the mind?

That's why the present is really a present from all creation.

Window of Imagination

The last four slides of her artwork are about the mystery of imagination. Everyone possesses a certain degree of imagination. The imagination manifests in various degrees in various people. Imagination is the ability to form a mental image of something that is not perceived through the five senses. It is the ability of the mind to build mental scenes, objects or events that do not exist, are not present, or have happened in the past.

Imagination has a great role and value in each one's life.

What mysteries do you love? Where do you get a sense of mystery?

In the end, it did reflect how Ailill saw the world and her place in it. The task, she told me, ended up being a fun adventure opening new doors and looking inside.

Chapter 16

Everyone Leaves a Legacy

"No legacy is as rich as honesty." ~ *William Shakespeare*

"Carve your name on hearts, not tombstones. A legacy is etched into the minds of others and the stories they share about you." *~Shannon L. Alder*

Ailill's memoirs wouldn't be complete if she didn't refer to her family legacy. What a privilege it is at this stage in her life that I get the privilege to articulate a story which might be a guidebook that hopefully, provides an accessible way to retrieve the past lives of her family member's unknown heroism. Hopefully by creating a tapestry of the connectedness of their lives it will mark the events and places which touched my soul and will bear witness to future generations.

Ailill story is about the O'Sullivan legacy. The idea behind the word legacy might intimate what is left after death, but it's not about death. Being reminded of death is a good thing, because death informs life. It gave Ailill a new perspective about what's important. It helped her decide the kind of life she wants to live and the kind of world she wants to live in. I found that even though her life brings tears of sadness and joy to my eyes, it rekindles the ageless spark of life that carries us all through time.

Ailill's legacy might seem mild compared to the accomplishments of the unsung heroes in her life which are her brother and her sisters. It is their lives that gave true meaning to the words, family legacy and portrays the contributions they made to future generations. Their sincerely humbly unwavering endurance during trying times shows what real hero's are made of. These family members are the real story; they knew how to make their life meaningful and fruitful. Their story will provide an ideal way for you to be your own fair witness to the healing and transforming power of what it means to be a family. Their story, the sharing, telling and hearing of the past is what allows Ailill to live her own legacy.

Her youngest sister, Quinn was her baby. Ailill remembers the day her mother brought her home from the hospital in a pink blanket and put her into her arms. Quinn will tell you that Ailill wasn't a very good sister. She agrees, Ailill felt so overly responsible for her that she was like her second mother. Ailill wrote in her diary about the awesome opportunity they had to be together last year for five weeks in Florida. It was the first time her brother and two sisters were all together in one place in nineteen years. They reminisced and shared stories as they laughed and cried about their experiences. This was such a magical, supreme blessing because out of the eight of them that gathered, seven of them have had life threatening emergencies and ambulance rides just this past year. Ailill's brother, shared with her before he passed last month that their trip was one of the best times of his life.

Quinn told Ailill for the first time how sad she was and what a gruesome experience it was for her when she left home and left her behind when she got married. She was eighteen but Quinn was only twelve years old. Their mother, Mary O'Sullivan had a sharp, gruff, and mean personality which worsened as the years past. As Ailill relived that experience through she little sister's eyes, her heart broke wide open with the sadness and abuse she had to endure. Quinn was able to vent and finally grieve what she had carried in her heart alone. It was her secret and she had not talked about it for fifty three years. It was devastating to learn that in her mind Ailill had left her alone. She had unknowingly abandoned her sister and she never knew. Her little sister has had the most challenging life of anyone Ailill have ever met. That is a generous statement considering all the people she has worked with. Both of her sisters suffered from the enmity at the hands their mother. They lived where she lived, worked for her, counseled her and took care of her until her very last breath. These are the family truths that weren't talked about. Both her sisters have had to grieve the loss of their own childhood and young adulthood, understanding a life they never had now as adult women. Their lives were entirely enmeshed with their mother's. Enmeshment is described as a relationship between two or more people in which each of their personal boundaries are permeable and unclear. This often happens on an emotional level. When one person's emotional state escalates it becomes contagious and everyone concerned begins to

160

demonstrate that same escalation. This is true whether those initial emotions are hysterical or joyful.

Both Ailill's sisters married lumber jacks from Idaho. Her little sister's husband, Manly fell fifty-six feet when working in New Mexico. Her three children were toddlers. Ailill flew to Albuquerque to be with her while he was in intensive care. They revived him three times during the ambulance ride. Her brother in law, Manly was to remain in a vegetative state for the next five years due to the trauma to his brain. A vegetative state is a nightmare because a person's brain can still feel pain but is unconscious to everything else around them. Quinn stayed by his side during all those years hoping and praying he would somehow wake up and recognize his family again. She would get so excited when she thought he moved his toe or when he would rarely utter a name. The courage and stamina it took to endure such a situation goes without saying but Ailill was in awe of her sister's devotion and commitment.

Ailill middle sister, Reagan to this day has a tough facade. People who are strong on the outside and have a tough exterior are often thought to be heartless, but delve a little deeper and you'll realize that these very people have a warm core. She even likes to fool herself by telling Ailill how tough she is. She was a power house of physical energy, claiming these days to be the "old gray mare, who aint what she used to be". She still moves fast, furiously working through anything that life throws at her. Courage is the ability to act on one's beliefs despite danger or disapproval. Ailill wrote in her diary describing Reagan, what came to mind was: daring, audacity, boldness, true grit, hardihood, heroism, and gallantry, among other things. Wow, she has held her in high esteem for a long time. Ailill knows her sister loves her but she hasn't always liked her. That is also a rare gift of Reagan's, you will always know what she thinks good and bad or right or wrong. Her second husband was a single father with four children. She had one daughter and they had another son together. Reagan raised these five children with love, giving them direction, always holding a high standard of obedience. They still consider her their mother. Reagan worked full time all of her life. In Ailill's opinion she was without a doubt the hardest working woman you will ever meet.

Reagan was always spiritually gifted. She is shy about her gift of clairvoyance. Ailill considers her a soul sister in that they can talk privately about anything whether it's paranormal or the everyday unusual. Reagan is a gifted artist. When Ailill went to visit her when she gave birth to her second son she had both her newborn child and her newborn granddaughter on her lap. Ailill had to ask which one was which. She was destined to be a mother. She tried natural childbirth even when giving birth late in life. Her heroic destiny will be forever present in all the children who have been blessed to have learned from and be loved by her.

Reagan and Quinn shared with Ailill last year what it was like for her and her family when Ailill would go to visit them in Idaho from California. In her sisters eyes she had a glamorous, rich life, which she did. Both of her sisters lived in trailers and their space was crowded. They shared how disgusting it was for Ailill to mention anything negative when she looked like she had everything and they had very little. The truth, Ailill was always uncomfortable and ashamed all those years. She didn't know how to tell them that some rich people are uncomfortable and lonely being rich, or at least being labeled rich. They just want to be thought of as normal, whatever that means.

The most important lesson to be learned concerning the four adult O'Sullivan siblings is that their relationships made it through the tests of time. They weathered the ups and down of life, from arguments, loss of jobs, money problems, teenagers, midlife crisis, health issues, and mothers-in-laws and death We were built with an integral strength that is based on *real connection.* Real connection has a force; an undeniable inner understanding of all that is right about being family. It's a mandate directed by the cosmos.

They all agreed when they discussed their children and grandchildren that they wished above all else that their offspring could and would experience the love and connection of family. That they would understand what we, as siblings, know from the deepest regions of our souls. Many of the younger O'Sullivan generation are estranged from one another but the brother and sisters will continue to pray, bless and hope that family relationships can heal and prosper. Hopefully, by looking past all

162

the blemishes, secrets, failures and brokenness everyone will see each other with a clear vision. Each of you just might meet the hearts of joy and the souls of pure love.

Since her illness her son, Dean Loughty and Ailill have been the closest they have ever been. Dean mentioned to her the other day how he felt that he was losing the two women he loved most in his life. He is currently going through a divorce after 32 years. Ailill and Dean cried together and talked about life from the deepest feelings in their hearts. Ailill used to tease him about being so guarded with his emotions. She would say, "Be careful honey you're getting close to a feeling". That is no longer true today. He is currently broken, deep to his soul, over the loss of his family, home, wife and lifestyle. Ailill's three grandsons are being amazingly strong through these trials. They are desperately trying to stay neutral as they love both their mother and their father so much. The breakdown of this family was a shock to everyone, especially her son and grandsons. From all appearances it seemed they were a close knit, happy family who fully lived within their Christian ideals.

Dean her son discovered his road to recovery through his church. He lovingly shares that his mother pushed him, preaching Al-Anon, Al-Ateen, Al-Atot, and he still became an alcoholic and an addict. He has over 25 years in recovery. For years he facilitated groups in his church, called Set Free. His books included passages from the bible with the explanations and references to the twelve steps. Ailill's heart is broken over the loss and grief her son is currently experiencing. Again, I see the truth that none of us can ever surmise we know about what goes on behind closed doors until we walk a mile in the other person's moccasins. The most challenging time is the scaring that builds up all during the healing process before it becomes a star. When we are in it, it feels like an endless dark eternity that could never possibly heal, but I am assured that healing does and will take place.

Ailill adult children and grandchildren are currently staring in their own lives. Despite their childhood tragedies all three became amazing productive citizens. Including her daughter, Kaitlyn before she passed, they were all earning a six figure income and all three were/are amazing parents. They love and protect their immediate families with passion and grace. They are all invested in

163

their children, through sports, school and college educations. Their children are successful. Ailill's grandchildren include three teenagers, four in college, one doctor, one respiratory therapist and a fireman. You've read her story. She did everything wrong but still got it right. The legacy of the O'Sullivan clan runs through their veins and none of them ever really knew Ailill or understood their inherited lineage of the everyday Viking and the stubborn Irish. Now they do and now she can say; "Be proud of what you are made of."

Of course, this doesn't mean everything in every moment is perfect. It just means that at its heart, there is a real regard, even admiration for each other that is the core of all relationships. It doesn't need to be manufactured or forced. It's just there. It's like a safety net of love.

Relationships will test everything we are individually and as a family, but they can also heal old wounds, and break our hearts wide open so we can discover a deeper more profound level of love.

Ultimately, time will tell. For real love will make you grow and show you what real togetherness/family is. It's the little things, you know? It's the kindnesses, the forgiveness, the mutual understanding and genuine affection for each other. It is about being proud of each other and at the end of the day trust grows by confiding in each other. It's about being able to truly be yourself, without fear of reprisals and that's eternal. All built on the mindful, loving understanding, that by working through our disconnection, we are creating a deeper and more lasting connection. This connection then becomes strong, bonded by trust and by forgiveness. Your love can be forged by experience like steel. This is real love. This kind of love is worth waiting for if you don't have it, and working to build if you do.

Ailill found that rereading her memoirs and allowing me to tell her story has been the greatest challenge of her life. She is standing naked in her honesty, sharing her hidden feelings, desperately wanting my family's acceptance and love. Ailill pulled the covers off the truth of who she is even with her fear of utter rejection.

Ailill challenged herself, taking off her masks facing her buried hurts, humiliations and blunders, openly confessing her shortcomings. She owned her own vision of the world. It was 12 months in God's waiting room that forced her give up the need to pretend that how you saw the world was important. At this point in her life she realized she couldn't be responsible for how others saw her. That being said, she confessed she was still shaking in her boots fearful that as others who read this you will only see the dark side of her family's trials and tribulations and none of her true accolades of pride, gratitude and love.

When she decided to do this project she asked my husband and a couple of her closest friends if they would publish copies of it to give to her family after she was dead. Their answer was not no, but "Hell no!" They asked her, "Why would you do that?" They lovingly pointed out to her that if she already felt abandoned then what was there to lose? She cautioned her husband and friends about the possibility of there being a book burning ceremony by certain members of my family.
No pressure here.

I have a family of the dearest most wonderful faithful friends you can imagine. I am supremely blessed. I am living my last year's staying close to where the love is. My understanding about life is that the people who were supposed to love me just didn't know how. Today I go where the love is. I have close relationships that are 50, 40, and 20 years old. I cherish the love of such loyal, supportive giving people. Everyone deserves to be remembered and looking death squarely in the face Ailill can now rest knowing she has left a beautiful legacy in these pages not only for her own family but maybe her story will bring light to yours.

Ailill's intention, when she agreed to this project was to give her family an honest rebuttal to all the horrific stories they have heard about her over the years as a mother and a grandmother. Being in God's waiting room has allowed her the privilege of introducing herself all over again to herself as well as her family. You only have to remember that every cell in your body has a memory so whoever you are look to those building blocks that have been reinforced generation upon generation. You can always learn something new from those that have gone before you.

About the Author

Mikki Alhart has had extensive experience as a counselor, consultant, educator and clinical supervisor for the past 40 years. In 1986 she received a degree at Boise State University as a trained Cognitive Behavior Therapist and Certified Alcohol and Drug Counselor .She is also certified as a Hypnotherapist and Master Reiki Teacher.

As a Human Resources Professional, she has worked as mental health counselor, and private practice and non-profit organizations in the field of Human Development. Currently she teaches alternative healing modalities at the Ventura College. She has over four decades of experience helping others integrate career, relationships, healing and spirit into everyday life.

Mrs. Alhart has studied extensively and explored many spiritual, psychological and self-help practices which she used to transform her own life. Her professional and spiritual path has included many cycles of healing and releasing which radiates to others with love and compassion. She has been blessed to work with literally thousands of people at the Salvation Army Rehabilitation Center, in San Diego California.

During the last seven years she opened an aura and charka imagining business using bio-feedback which gives her clients visible proof of their own energy field. Throughout her career Mikki's main focus has always been to support and care for the community at large. Being able to incorporate several complimentary modalities of healing allows her to genuinely enjoy creating a feeling of well-being for others and why she has chosen to work in a variety of fields. Mikki currently offers different education programs which include Aura/Chakra analysis and healing through Reiki along with other intuitive healing modalities.

Mikki is also an accomplished artist and has been a member of several art associations on the Central Coast.

Alhart's other books; Taming the Beast Named Habit and The Addiction Monster Doesn't live here Anymore are being used by various organizations including Good Samaritan, Adolescent Group Homes and other Recovery Intuitions.

Glossary

A

Abandonment:
Fear often stems from childhood loss. This loss could be related to a traumatic event, such as the loss of a parent through death or divorce.

Abstract Art:
Abstract art is art that does not attempt to represent an accurate depiction of a visual reality but instead use shapes, colors, forms and gestural marks to achieve its effect.

Acceptance:
Acceptance in human psychology is a person's assent to the reality of a situation, recognizing a process or condition (often a negative or uncomfortable situation) without attempting to change it or protest it. The concept is close in meaning to acquiescence, derived from the Latin acquiēscere (to find rest in).

Accountability:
To be responsible means to be answerable for something within one's power or control. To be accountable means to be subject to giving an account or having the obligation to report, explain or justify something.

Addiction:
Is a term that means compulsive physiological need for and use of a habit-forming substance (like heroin or nicotine), characterized by tolerance and well-defined physiological symptoms upon withdrawal; it has also been used more broadly to refer to compulsive use of a substance known by the user

Ah Ha Moments:
A moment of sudden realization, inspiration, insight, recognition, or comprehension.

Al-Anon:
The Al-Anon Family Groups are a fellowship of relatives and friends of alcoholics who share their experience, strength and hope in order to solve their common problems. We believe alcoholism is a family illness, and that changed attitudes can aid recovery.

Alcoholism:
Alcohol abuse disorder refers to a long-term addiction to alcohol. A person with this condition does not know when or how to stop drinking. They spend a lot of time thinking about alcohol, and they cannot control how much they consume, even if it is causing serious problems at home, work, and financially.

Alternative Healing:
These forms of alternative medicine are built upon a complete system of ideas and practice and may have evolved in Western or non-Western cultures. Examples include Ayurveda, Chiropractic, Homeopathy, Naturopathic medicine, Osteopathy, and Traditional Chinese medicine.

Anorexia:
Anorexia nervosa is a psychological condition that involves an eating disorder. Symptoms include a very low body mass index (BMI), a refusal to eat, and attempts to lose weight, even when body mass index is very low.

Ashamed:
Feeling shame; distressed or embarrassed by feelings of guilt, foolishness, or disgrace: He felt ashamed for having spoken so cruelly. Unwilling or restrained because of fear of shame, ridicule, or disapproval.

Attribute of God:
These terms describe God's attributes, or characteristics. Omnipotence means God is all-powerful. ... This means God knows everything, including the past and future. There is nothing God is unaware of. Omnipresence means God is everywhere at the same time.

Aura:

The Color Of Your Aura Is Reflective Of Your Physical, Emotional, And Spiritual Health. A person who is healthy, self-confident, and positive, though, tends to have a bright, light aura that other people can sense, even if they can't see it

Authentic Self:

Being your true authentic self means what you say in life aligns with what your actions. It is about being true to yourself through your thoughts, words, and actions, and having these three areas match each other.

Automatic Writing:

Automatic writing or psychograph is a claimed psychic ability allowing a person to produce written words without consciously writing. The words purportedly arise from a subconscious, spiritual or supernatural source. Scientists and skeptics consider automatic writing to be the result of the ideomotor effect and even proponents of automatic writing admit it has been the source of innumerable cases of self-delusion. Automatic writing is not the same thing as free writing.

B

Bio-Feedback:

One technique can help you gain more control over these normally involuntary functions. It's called biofeedback, and the therapy is used to help prevent or treat conditions, including migraine headaches, chronic pain, incontinence, and high blood pressure. During biofeedback, you're connected to electrical sensors that help you receive information about your body.

Bio-Locate:

Bilocation, or sometimes multilocation, is an alleged psychic or miraculous ability wherein an individual or object is located (or appears to be located) in two distinct places at the same time.

Blarney Stone:
The Blarney Stone (Irish:
Cloch na Blarnan) is a block of Carboniferous limestone built into
the battlements of Blarney Castle, Blarney, about 8 kilometers (5
miles) from Cork, Ireland. ... The word blarney has come to mean
"clever, flattering, or coaxing talk".

Blessings:
Is a noun The act or words of a person who blesses A special
favor, mercy, or benefit: The blessings of liberty. A favor or gift
bestowed by God, thereby bringing happiness... praise; devotion;
worship, especially grace said before a meal:

Body, Mind, Soul:
Your mind is affected by your spirit, and vice versa. Your body is
affected by your mind and your spirit and vice versa. ... Mind,
Body, Spirit means that our well-being comes from not just
physical health, but from mental health and spiritual health as well

Buddha:
The teaching founded by the Buddha is known, in English, as
Buddhism. ... A Buddha is one who has attained Bodhi; and by
Bodhi is meant wisdom, an ideal state of intellectual and ethical
perfection which can be achieved by man through purely human
means. The term Buddha literally means enlightened one, a
knower.

Bulimia:
A syndrome in which the symptoms of both bulimia and anorexia
nervosa are present, characterized by distorted body image,
excessive weight loss, and use of forced vomiting to compensate
for periods of binge eating.

C

Carl Jung:
Was a Swiss psychiatrist and founder of analytical psychology. He is best known for his theories of the Collective Unconscious, including the concept of archetypes, and the use of synchronicity in psychotherapy.

Chakra:
Chakras are the circular vortexes of energy that are placed in seven different points on the spinal column, and all the seven chakras are connected to the various organs and glands within the body. These chakras are responsible for disturbing the life energy, which is also known as Qi or Praana.

Chakra Balance:
Chakra balancing is based on the ancient Indian belief in a series of seven chakras, or energy centers. Chakra is the Sanskrit word for wheel. ... Chakra balancing is believed to promote health by maximizing the flow of energy in the body, much as a tune-up enables a car to operate at peak efficiency.

Channeling:
The practice of channeling — a person's body being taken over by a spirit for the purpose of communication — has been around for millennia. ... Channeling is the belief that a person's body has being taken over by a spirit for the purpose of imparting wisdom.

Challenged:
If you say that someone is challenged in a particular way, you mean that they have a disability in that area. Challenged is often combined with inappropriate words for humorous effect.

Character Defects:
Fault, failing, weakness, flaw, shortcoming, and inadequacy are all synonyms for the word defect. Character refers to the mental and moral qualities of an individual. Thus, the ubiquitous phrase in the recovery world defects of character implies moral and psychological flaws and failings in an individual.

Characteristic:
Being a feature that helps to distinguish a person or thing; distinctive: heard my friend's characteristic laugh; the stripes that are characteristic of the zebra. A feature that helps to identify, tell apart, or describe recognizably; a distinguishing mark or trait

Clairvoyant:
In French, "clairvoyant" literally means "clear-seeing," mentally or optically. The term made a brief appearance in English in the 17th century, as an adjective suggesting a keen sense of perception, but it did not become firmly established in the language until the 19th century.

Clan:
A clan is a group of people united by actual or perceived kinship and descent. ... The word clan is derived from the Gaelic clan meaning "children" or "progeny"; it is not from the word for "family" in either Irish or Scottish Gaelic.

Co-Dependence:
A psychological condition or a relationship in which a person is controlled or manipulated by another who is affected with a pathological condition (such as an addiction to alcohol or heroin) broadly: dependence on the nees of or control by another.

Coincidence:
A coincidence is something that's not planned or arranged but seems like it is. Technically, a coincidence is an occurrence of events that happen at the same time by total accident –
like you and a kid from your class at school both visit the Grand Canyon on the same day. Weird.

Collective Consciousness:
Collective consciousness (sometimes collective conscience or conscious) is a fundamental sociological concept that refers to the set of shared beliefs, ideas, attitudes, and knowledge that are common to a social group or society. Universal mind or universal consciousness is a concept that tries to address the underlying essence of all being and becoming in the universe.

Consciousness:
Is the state or quality of sentience or awareness of internal or external existence. ... Despite the difficulty in definition, many philosophers believe that there is a broadly shared underlying intuition about Consequential
Consequential what consciousness is.

Convalescence:
Is the gradual recovery of health and strength after illness or injury. It refers to the later stage of an infectious disease or illness when the patient recovers and returns to previous health, but may continue to be a source of infection to others even if feeling better.

Cosmic:
If it has to do with the universe, it's cosmic. The planets, for instance, are cosmic bodies. When you use the word cosmic to describe something big, you often use it with the word, proportions. A big mistake might be an error of cosmic proportions.

Courage:
In Middle English, courage referred to "what is in one's mind or thoughts." Today, anyone with courage has only fearless feats and courageous acts in mind. Having courage means acting when others are afraid of the danger, or simply acting without fear of failure.

Covenant:
Literally, a contract. In the Bible, an agreement between God and his people, in which God makes promises to his people and, usually, requires certain conduct from them. In the Old Testament, God made agreements with Noah, Abraham, and Moses.

<u>Cross Over – Transition</u>:
A parallel universe, also known as a parallel dimension, alternate universe or alternate reality, is a hypothetical self-contained plane of existence, co-existing with one's own. The sum of all potential parallel universes that constitute reality is often called a "multiverse". Refers to the dying person having finished all business and made peace with others before his/her death and implies being at peace with his/her own death. It further refers to the manner of dying: not by violence, an accident or a fearsome disease, not by foul means and without much pain.

D

<u>Death</u>:
The irreversible cessation of all vital functions especially as indicated by permanent stoppage of the heart, respiration, and brain activity: The end of life.

<u>Deity</u>:
The word deity means "divine nature." It was coined by Saint Augustine, a theologian whose writings were very influential in the shaping of Western Christianity. Deity comes from the Latin word for "god":Deus. The divine nature of deities is believed to be immortal goodness and powerfulness.

<u>Depression</u>:
Depression (major depressive disorder) is a common and serious medical illness that negatively affects how you feel the way you think and how you act. Fortunately, it is also treatable. Depression causes feelings of sadness and/or a loss of interest in activities once enjoyed. It can lead to a variety of emotional and physical problems and can decrease a person's ability to function at work and at home.

<u>Destiny</u>:
Destiny is what's meant to be, what's written in the stars, your inescapable fate. A noun meaning fate, destiny is synonymous with other nouns like divine decree, fortune, and serendipity. There's no avoiding destiny — it's going to happen no matter what you do.

Devotion:
Devotional literature (also called devotionals or Christian living literature) is religious writing that is neither doctrinal nor theological, but designed for individuals to read for their personal edification and spiritual formation

Dimensions:
When someone mentions "different dimensions," we tend to think of things like parallel universes – alternate realities that exist parallel to our own, but where things work or happened differently. ... The first dimension, as already noted, is that which gives it length

Divine:
Divine basically means relating to, coming from, or like God Divine also has an old-fashioned and informal meaning of being very good or pleasing. Addressed, appropriated, or devoted to God or a god; religious; sacred: divine worship. Proceeding from God or a god: divine laws; divine guidance. Godlike; characteristic of or befitting a deity: divine magnanimity.

DNA:
Deoxyribonucleic acid:
an extremely long macromolecule that is the main component of chromosomes and is the material that transfers genetic characteristics in all life forms, constructed of two nucleotide strands coiled around each other in a ladder like. Humans, genes vary in size from a few hundred DNA bases to more than 2 million bases. The Human Genome Project estimated that humans have between 20,000 and 25,000 genes. Every person has two copies of each gene, one inherited from each parent.

Drug Addiction:
Addiction is defined as a chronic, relapsing disorder characterized by compulsive drug seeking, continued use despite harmful consequences, and long-lasting changes in the brain.

E

Eccentric:
Eventually it came to describe people who were a little kooky, both as an adjective and as a noun, too: an eccentric is an unconventional, odd person. Think of them as following a slightly different orbit from the rest of society.

Eclectic:
The definition of eclectic is something that is made up of various sources or styles. An example of eclectic is the taste in music of a person who enjoys listening to country, hip hop, gospel and classical music.

Emergence:
Emerge, emanate, issue mean to come forth. Emerge is used of coming forth from a place shut off from view, or from concealment, or the like, into sight and notice:
The sun emerges from behind the clouds

Empaths:
Empaths are highly sensitive individuals, who have a keen ability to sense what people around them are thinking and feeling. Psychologists may use the term empath to describe a person that experiences a great deal of empathy, often to the point of taking on the pain of others at their own expense.

Empathy versus Sympathy:
Sympathy is a shared feeling, usually of sorrow, pity or compassion for another person. You show concern for another person when you feel sympathy for them. Empathy is stronger than sympathy. It is the ability to put you in the place of another and understand someone else's feelings by identifying with them.

Endocrinologist:
Endocrinologists have the training to diagnose and treat hormone imbalances and problems by helping to restore the normal balance of hormones in the body. The common diseases and disorders of the endocrine system that endocrinologists deal with include diabetes mellitus and thyroid disorders.

Energy Medicine:
Energy therapies are healing techniques that use "energy" to treat symptoms and disease. ... Energy therapies are alternative therapies that aim to create a state of balance, health and peace in a person. An underlying theory to energy therapies involves energy blockages or imbalances that lead to illness and disease. Other holistic methods of healing include acupuncture, acupressure, and even crystal healing. Further, additional energy healing techniques include scanning the field, still hands, magnetizing, energy pump, and Celtic weave. Two of the most popular are pranic healing and reiki healing.

Enmeshment:
What Enmeshed Parenting Means to Your Children. Unfortunately, being an enmeshed parent means that your children may grow up learning things from your behavior and focus that you never intended. This can include: They may grow up feeling responsible for others' feelings while ignoring responsibility for their own.

Enmity:
Enmity and its synonyms "hostility," animosity, and animus all indicate deep-seated dislike or ill will. Enmity (which derives from an Anglo-French word meaning "enemy") suggests true hatred, either overt or concealed. Hostility implies strong, open enmity that shows itself in attacks or aggression.

Essence:
Essence is defined as the core nature or most important qualities of a person or thing. An example of essence is what is captured of someone's personality in a good photograph. The definition of an essence is a concentrated form of a flavor. The essence of being human. The more I listen to what they are trying to say, the clearer it becomes that in essence they are talking mostly about embracing the essence of being human. Their life experience has brought them to a few conclusions as to what the essence of being human is. Humans are social animals.

Estrangements:
The adjective estranged suggests a loss of affection, a turning away from someone. When a couple separates, we often refer to them as estranged — or no longer together. The word estranged is an unfriendly word with a negative connotation.

Ethereal Body
Etheric cords (sometimes referred to as ethereal cords, energy cords, and ribbons) are energy structures that connect to your energy bodies (aura, chakras, etc.). They extend out of you and connect with other people, places, animals and even objects. The etheric body, in the vast majority of humans, is the vehicle or the instrument of astral energy. It gives vitality, health, life and organization to the physical body. It steps energies from the higher bodies down into our physical consciousness.

Expressionism:
Expressionism is a modernist movement, initially in poetry and painting, originating in Germany at the beginning of the 20th century. ... Expressionist artists have sought to express the meaning of emotional experience rather than physical reality. Expressionism developed as an avant-garde style before the First World War.

F

Faith:
"Now faith is the substance of things hoped for, the evidence of things not seen" Hebrews 11:
1. Faith is the connecting power into the spiritual realm, which links us with God and makes Him become a tangible reality to the sense perceptions of a person. Faith is the basic ingredient to begin a relationship with God.

Fanatical:
If you are excessively enthusiastic about something — a sports team, an actor, your religion, saving the whales, a certain brand of chocolate — then you are fanatical about it. Fanatical comes from the word fanatic, which itself came from the Latin fanaticus, meaning "mad" or "inspired by a deity.

Fantasy Thinking:
A fantasy is something you imagine, which might involve dragons, unicorns, or an imaginary best friend. If you live in a fantasy world, you're not worrying much about reality — pleasant, maybe, but not very practical. Fantasy is dreams and imagination. ... But sometimes a fantasy is all you need."

Forgiveness:
Psychologists generally define forgiveness as a conscious, deliberate decision to release feelings of resentment or vengeance toward a person or group who has harmed you, regardless of whether they actually deserve your forgiveness. Forgiveness does not mean forgetting, nor does it mean condoning or excusing offenses.

G

Generation:
A generation is "all of the people born and living at about the same time, regarded collectively." It can also be described as, "The average period, generally considered to be about thirty years, during which children are born and grow up, become adults, and begin to have children of their own"

Gossip:
The definition of a gossip is someone who reveals personal information about others. A friend who passes on the secrets of other friends, but asks you not to tell is an example of a gossip. Gossip is defined as the private information about others shared in conversation or print.

Gratitude:
Gratitude means thanks and appreciation. ... Gratitude, which rhymes with "attitude," comes from the Latin word gratus, which means "thankful, pleasing." When you feel gratitude, you're pleased by what someone did for you and also pleased by the results. Unlike indebtedness, you're not anxious about having to pay it back. Gratitude is a personality trait, a mood, and an emotion. As an emotion, gratitude is a feeling of happiness that

comes from appreciation. While under a grateful mood, grateful emotions are more likely to traffic.

Grief:
Grief means intense sorrow. You feel grief if something terribly sad happens, like if your dog dies or if your childhood sweetheart breaks up with you. The word grief comes from the Latin word gravare, which means to make heavy. Gravare itself comes from the Latin word gravis, which means weighty. You will probably react to learning of the loss with numbed disbelief.

Seven stages of grief:
Shock & Denial
Pain & Guilt
Anger & Bargaining
Depression, Reflection, Loneliness
The Upward Turn
Reconstruction & Moving Through
Acceptance & Hope

Guardian Angel:
A guardian angel is an angel assigned to protect and guide a particular person or group. Belief in both the East and the West is that guardian angels serve to protect whichever person God assigns them to, and present prayer to God on that person's behalf.

H

Healing:
(See Spiritual Healing)

Heroism:
When you think of heroism, you might think of great acts of bravery, such as rushing into burning buildings and facing danger in battle. ... As someone who shows great courage and valor is referred to as a hero, their actions are considered to be acts of Holistic.

Holistic:
A holistic approach means thinking about the big picture. ... In a medical setting, holistic refers to addressing the whole person, including their physical, mental, and emotional health, while taking social factors into consideration.

181

Hospice:
Hospice is for patients whose condition is such that a doctor would not be surprised if the patient died within the next six months. This doesn't mean the patient is going to die in the next six months--it simply means that he or she has a condition that makes dying a realistic possibility.

I

Imagination:
Imagination is the ability to produce and simulate novel objects, peoples and ideas in the mind without any immediate input of the senses. ... The active types of imagination include integration of modifiers, and mental rotation. Imagined images, both novel and recalled, are seen with the "mind's eye".

Impressionism:
Often capitalized, a theory or practice in painting especially among French painters of about 1870 of depicting the natural appearances of objects by means of dabs or strokes of primary unmixed colors in order to simulate actual reflected light

Inspiration:
Inspire means to excite, encourage, or breathe life into. Inspire comes from the Latin word that means to inflame or to blow in to. When you inspire something, it is as if you are blowing air over a low flame to make it grow. A film can be inspired by a true story.

Intuition:
Quick and ready insight.
a :immediate apprehension or cognition.
b :knowledge or conviction gained by intuition.
c :the power or faculty of attaining to direct knowledge or cognition without evident rational thought and inference.

J

Johari Windows:
The Johari Window is the psychological model developed by Joseph Luft and Harrington Ingham that talk about the relationship and mutual understanding between the group members. ... Hidden Self: This quadrant of the Johari window shows the state of an individual known to him but not known to the others.

Journal:
A journal is a written record of incidents, experiences, and ideas. Also known as a personal journal, notebook, diary, and log. Writers often keep journals to record observations and explore ideas that may eventually be developed into more formal essays, articles, and stories.

Journey:
From the Old French journée, meaning a "day's work or travel," journey doubles as both noun and verb. The noun simply refers to a voyage; the verb is the act of taking that voyage. ... Either way, you should always remember that life is a journey, not a destination.

K

Krishna:
Krishna was born in prison to devout parents – Devaki and Vasudeva. At the time of his birth, his life was in danger because the tyrant Kamsa was seeking to kill him. It had been foretold that Kamsa would be killed by Devaki's eighth child. ... Some worship Sri Krishna as the ideal child of innocence.

L

Legacy:
It surprises me how many leaders don't spend enough time thinking about their legacy – what they will leave behind for the organization and the people they serve. Webster's dictionary defines legacy as, "anything handed down from the past, as from an ancestor or predecessor." he dictionary would define Legacy as a gift or a bequest, that is handed down, endowed or conveyed from one person to another. It is something descendible one comes into possession of that is transmitted, inherited or received from a predecessor.

M

Manifestation:
A manifestation is the public display of emotion or feeling, or something theoretical made real. Manifestation's origins are in religion and spirituality because if something spiritual becomes real, it is said to be a manifestation. The word's usage has spread to include all aspects of life.

Meditation:
1: To engage in contemplation or reflection He meditated long and hard before announcing his decision.
2: to engage in mental exercise (such as concentration on one's breathing or repetition of a mantra) for the purpose of reaching a heightened level of spiritual awareness. Christian meditation is a form of prayer in which a structured attempt is made to become aware of and reflect upon the revelations of God. ... Christian meditation is the process of deliberately focusing on specific thoughts (such as a bible passage) and reflecting on their meaning in the context of the love of God. The goal of meditation is to go beyond the mind and experience our essential nature—which is described as peace, happiness, and bliss. But as anyone who has tried to meditate knows, the mind itself is the biggest obstacle standing between ourselves and this awareness.

Meditative Practice:
Is an approach to training the mind, similar to the way that fitness is an approach to training the body. ... And different meditation practices require different mental skills. It's extremely difficult for a beginner to sit for hours and think of nothing or have an "empty mind." Types of meditation
Loving-kindness meditation. With the many types of meditation to try, there should be one to suit most individuals. ...
Body scan or progressive relaxation. ...
Mindfulness meditation. ...
Breath awareness meditation. ...
Kundalini yoga. ...
Zen meditation. ...
Transcendental Meditation.

Medium:
Attempts to communicate with the dead and other living human beings, aka spirits, have been documented back to early human history. The story of the Witch of Endor (In the most recent edition of the NIV witch is rendered medium in the passage) tells of one who raised the spirit of the deceased prophet Samuel to allow the Hebrew king Saul to question his former mentor about an upcoming battle, as related in the Books of Samuel in the Jewish Tanakh (the basis of the Old Testament).

Melchizedek:
And Melchizedek king of Salem brought out bread and wine: and he was [is] the priest of the most high God. And he blessed him, and said, 'Blessed be Abram to the most high God, possessor of heaven and earth, And blessed be the most high God, which hath delivered thine enemies into thy hand'. According to the writer of Hebrews (7:13-17) Jesus is considered a priest in the order of Melchizedek because, like Melchizedek, Jesus was not a descendant of Aaron, and thus would not qualify for the Jewish priesthood under the Law of Moses.

Memoirs:
A memoir from French: (mémoire:memoria,) meaning memory or reminiscence is a collection of memories that an individual writes about moments or events, both public or private, that took place in the subject's/person's life. ... The author of a memoir may be referred to as a memoirist or a memorialist.

Metaphysical:
Metaphysics is a type of philosophy or study that uses broad concepts to help define reality and our understanding of it. Metaphysical studies generally seek to explain inherent or universal elements of reality which are not easily discovered or experienced in our everyday life. Metaphysics is not the branch of philosophy that explains physical phenomena using reason and logic in a way that falls outside the bounds of either religion or science' rather it is a philosophical science which deals with transcendental concepts such as being, one, true and good which in its simplest form is 'being ...

Mindfulness: also involves acceptance, meaning that we pay attention to our thoughts and feelings without judging them— without believing, for instance, that there's a "right" or "wrong" way to think or feel in a given moment.

Modalities:
A modality is the way or mode in which something exists or is done. You might often see it used with reference to diagnostic modality, which is the way in which a disease or illness is diagnosed by a doctor.

Moral Compass:
Moral compass (plural moral compasses) (ethics) An inner sense which distinguishes what is right from what is wrong, functioning as a guide (like the needle of a compass) for morally appropriate behavior.

Muhammad:
Is the prophet and founder of Islam. Born in Mecca in 570, most of his early life was spent as a merchant. At age 40, he began to have revelations from Allah that became the basis for the Koran and the foundation of Islam. By 630 he had unified most of Arabia under a single religion.

Multigenerational:
Consisting of, relating to, or involving more than one generation (as of a family) multigenerational households Farm life is unique because of its closeness to the land, the need for family members to work together, the multigenerational involvement, and the sense of family entrepreneurship.

Muse:

As a noun, it means a person — especially a woman — who is a source of artistic inspiration. In mythology, the Muses were nine goddesses who symbolized the arts and sciences. Today, a muse is a person who serves as an artist's inspiration. The definition of a muse is a spirit or source that inspires an artist. An example of muse is someone having a thought about the origin of life. An example of muse is the character Kira from the movie Xanadu.

N

Negative Energy:

The electrons in the orbits have negative energy. If energy of a particle is positive, it can deliver the energy to other system. If it is negative, it requires some energy to come out of its state. ... So, negative energy means the level is below the ground state. It is when a person absorbs, either subconsciously or consciously, unhealthy and negative energy. ... Your Negative Energy absorption goes up. Humans are feeling and emitting beings, so there is always opportunity to share energy, both positive and negative.

O

Old Crone:

The Mother represents ripeness, fertility, sexuality, fulfillment, stability, power and life represented by the full moon; The Crone represents wisdom, repose, death, and endings represented by the waning moon. The Crone is also an archetypal figure, a Wise Woman.

Omnipotent :

If you want to describe someone who can do absolutely anything, reach for the adjective omnipotent. Omnipotent comes from the Latin words for total (omni) and power (potent). Omnipotent is frequently used for deities, but can apply to any exaggerated description of power. All-powerful, almighty. Words Related to omnipotent. Great, sovereign, supreme, towering, transcendent.

187

Omnipresent:
Omnipresence means all-present. This term means that God is capable of being everywhere at the same time. It means his divine presence encompasses the whole of the universe. There is no location where he does not inhabit.

Omniscient:
To be omniscient is to know everything. This often refers to a special power of God. If you combine the Latin roots omnis (meaning "all") and scientia (meaning "knowledge"), you'll get omniscient, meaning "knowledge of all." Many religions have a god who is all-powerful and omniscient.

P

Perception:
The act or faculty of perceiving, or apprehending by means of the senses or of the mind; cognition; understanding. Immediate or intuitive recognition or appreciation, as of moral, psychological, or aesthetic qualities; insight; intuition; discernment:
an artist of rare perception.

Personality Quotient: For most people, emotional intelligence (EQ) is more important than one's intelligence (IQ) in attaining success in their lives and careers. As individuals our success and the success of the profession today depend on our ability to read other people's signals and react appropriately to them. Therefore, each one of us must develop the mature emotional intelligence skills required to better understand, empathize and negotiate with other people — particularly as the economy has become more global. Otherwise, success will elude us in our lives and careers.

Pharmaceuticals:
Pharmaceutical products – more commonly known as medicines or drugs – are a fundamental component of both modern and traditional medicine. It is essential that such products are safe, effective, and of good quality, and are prescribed and used rationally.

Philosophies:
Philosophy is a way of thinking about the world, the universe, and society. It works by asking very basic questions about the nature of human thought, the nature of the universe, and the connections between them. The ideas in philosophy are often general and abstract.

Phobic:
What is a phobia? A phobia is a type of anxiety disorder. It is an extreme form of fear or anxiety triggered by a particular situation (such as going outside) or object (such as spiders), even when there is no danger. Occurs in technical usage in psychiatry to construct words that describe irrational, abnormal, unwarranted, persistent, or disabling fear as a mental disorder (e.g. agoraphobia)

Physics:
The dictionary definition of physics is "the study of matter, energy, and the interaction between them", but what that really means is that physics is about asking fundamental questions and trying to answer them by observing and experimenting.

Physic:
A psychic is a person who claims to use extrasensory perception (ESP) to identify information hidden from the normal senses, particularly involving telepathy or clairvoyance, or who performs acts that are apparently inexplicable by natural laws.

Premonition:
Some people claim to have premonitions, such as a dream about a friend they haven't seen in years the night before the friend dies. A premonition is a warning that comes in advance, or a feeling that something is going to happen. Like the synonym foreboding, a premonition usually refers to something bad or harmful. Synonyms for premonition are: anticipation, foreknowledge. feel, insight, intuition, omen, portent, sign. Impression, suspicion. agitation, alarm (also alarum), anxiety, anxiousness, apprehension, apprehensiveness, care, concern, disquiet, doubt, dread, fear, misgiving, nervousness, perturbation, unease, uneasiness, worry.

Psychobabble:
Writing or talk using jargon from psychiatry or psychotherapy without particular accuracy or relevance. With the advent of popular psychology magazines, self-help books, and an increasing interest in therapy, psychology has become a part of popular culture, and people commonly incorporate psychological terms into their conversations.

R

Realism:
An approach to philosophy that regards external objects as the most fundamentally real things, with perceptions or ideas as secondary. In the arts is generally the attempt to represent subject matter truthfully, without artificiality and avoiding artistic conventions, or implausible, exotic, and supernatural elements.

Reality:
is the state of things as they actually exist, as opposed to an idealistic or notional idea of them. Reality includes everything that is and has been, whether or not it is observable or comprehensible. A still broader definition includes that which has existed, exists, or will exist.

Recovery:
In most of life, "being in recovery" means a person is making progress even though s/he isn't "cured." But too often, being "in recovery" has come to mean something different:
That they are on what they declare is the right path.

Reiki:
Reiki is a therapy often described as palm healing or hands-on-body healing in which a practitioner places hands lightly on or over a patient's body to facilitate the patient's process of healing. Reiki combines the Japanese and Chinese word-characters of "rei" (spiritual or supernatural) and "ki" (vital energy). The spiritual healing art of Reiki works by channeling positive energy into your body, with Reiki masters and practitioners typically placing their hands on the affected areas of the body that need a boost, offering this energy and your body takes in the energy where most needed.

Reiki Master:
There are three levels or degrees of Reiki, which are achieved by successive initiations. The first degree opens the energy channel and permits the student to channel Reiki mainly at the physical level, both for himself and for others. It consists of one initiation in the Usui Tibetan system.

Religion:
A set of beliefs concerning the cause, nature, and purpose of the universe, especially when considered as the creation of a superhuman agency or agencies, usually involving devotional and ritual observances, and often containing a moral code governing the conduct of human affairs.

Reminiscent: reminding you of someone or something else: similar to something else. Literary + formal: thinking about the Past: having many thoughts of the past.

S

Sacred Connection:
A sacred relationship is a relationship in which we are inspired to see the Divine in another person. To experience Oneness through the union of two. We become ready for this sacred relationship at a very particular time in our lives - a time when we awaken to the sacredness within ourselves.

Scar:
Your Scars are Symbols of your Strength. Don't ever be ashamed of the scars life has left you with. A scar means the hurt is over and the wound is closed. It means you conquered the pain, learned a lesson, grew stronger, and moved forward.
Self-awareness: Self-awareness is the ability to accurately recognize your: emotions, strengths, limitations, actions and understand how these affect others around you.

Self-Care versus Selfish:
Selfish is choosing to consistently only think of your own needs and wants. Selfishness never yields joy, peace or love. ... Self Care is choosing to honor your inner wants and needs in order to fulfill your potential, discover your purpose and experience joy. Sometimes that requires putting yourself ahead of someone else.

Self-Esteem:
In psychology, the term self-esteem is used to describe a person's overall sense of self-worth or personal value. In other words, how much you appreciate and like yourself. Self-esteem is often seen as a personality trait, which means that it tends to be stable and enduring.

Serendipity:
If you find good things without looking for them, serendipity — unexpected good luck — has brought them to you. ... The meaning of the word, good luck in finding valuable things unintentionally, refers to the fairy tale characters who were always making discoveries through chance.

Shadow Side:
What is the 'shadow' self according to psychology? The 'shadow' is the side of your personality that contains all the parts of yourself that you don't want to admit to having. It is at first an unconscious side. It is only through effort to become self-aware that we recognize our shadow.

Shamanism:
a religion practiced by indigenous peoples of far northern Europe and Siberia that is characterized by belief in an unseen world of gods, demons, and ancestral spirits responsive only to the shamans also: any similar religion Shamanic Cleansing, on the other hand, is a holistic and intensive practice where we delve into the invisible realm of Mind and Spirit in order to correct imbalances. We work with Shamanic Elders who help us open up a healing space in order to explore these profound and sacred invisible realms.

Shame:
Shame has been proven to be toxic to humans. Shame is a painful feeling that's a mix of regret, self-hate, and dishonor. A good person would feel shame if they cheated on a test or did something mean to a friend. ... People also often say, "That's a shame," when something bad happens — meaning it's sad or a pity.

Short Comings:
a weakness in someone's character:
a personal fault or failing. :
A bad feature:
a flaw or defect in something.

Skeptics:
1: an attitude of doubt or a disposition to incredulity either in general or toward a particular object.
2a: the doctrine that true knowledge or knowledge in a particular area is uncertain.
2b: the method of suspended judgment, systematic doubt, or criticism characteristic of skeptics. The attitude of doubting knowledge claims set forth in various areas.

Soul:
The noun soul can mean an individual human being, but it can also mean essence of a human being. If you believe the soul is immortal, you believe that even when your physical body dies, some other part of you lives on.

Soul Retrieval:
Shamanic healing techniques have been successfully used for thousands of years to help people miraculously let go of old trauma, emotional wounds, hurts, self-sabotaging patterns, energetic blocks, illnesses, diseases and more. Soul retrieval is one of the most effective and well-known shamanic healing practices to restore lost life force. The loss of life force is known as soul loss, and this can take place when we suffer a trauma, have an accident, separate from a partner, experience the death of a loved one, or go through a pervasive period of difficult circumstances.

Spirit:

Spirit comes from the Latin word for "breath," and like breath, spirit is considered a fundamental part of being alive. ... We also use spirit to mean "the general mood or intent," like when you tell your former enemy, "I approach you in the spirit of. The Holy Spirit is referred to as the Lord and Giver of Life in the Nicene Creed. He is The Creator Spirit, present before the creation of the universe and through his power everything was made in Jesus Christ, by God the Father. Christian hymns such as Veni Creator Spiritus reflects this belief.

Spirit Team:

There are many types of spirit guides that are able to provide advice and assistance in any situation. Be confident that the right guide will present itself at exactly the right time in order to help you in the best way possible for your life without hurting anyone else. Spirit guides can be labeled as Archangels, Angels, Guardian Angels and Guides, Goddesses, Ascended Masters and Enlightened Beings, Ancestors, Spirit Animals, Elemental Energies (Sylphs, Undines, Salamanders, and Gnomes), or something residing upon the earth such as a tree, mountain, or body of water. Anything that holds energy has the ability to use that energy to communicate impressions, feelings, thoughts and healing.

Spiritual healing:

is about finding a connection to something greater than yourself, be it friendship, community, a sense of virtue or meaning, God, a higher power or some sense of higher truth, beauty or sacredness in life.

Spiritually Gifted:

It's a specified skill God placed inside of you which requires little or no practice to perfect. An individual displays a strong and natural inclination/proclivity towards this gift and he/she is just a raw talent in a certain area.

Subconscious:
Is a psychic activity just below the level of awareness. The subconscious is the part of our mind that is not in current awareness. It is the part of our consciousness that is not being focused on and is lying dormant. ... This storage is known as the subconscious, the term being coined by Pierre Janet. When you fall asleep, it is your conscious mind that is sleeping. However, your subconscious mind will never fall asleep. ... And that simply means that it is your unconscious mind that is solely responsible for your dreams.

Symbolism:
Symbolism is the use of symbols to signify ideas and qualities, by giving them symbolic meanings that are different from their literal sense. Symbolism can take different forms. Generally, it is an object representing another, to give an entirely different meaning that is much deeper and more significant.

T

Tai Chi:
The essential principles include mind integrated with the body; control of movements and breathing; generating internal energy, mindfulness, song (loosening 松) and jing (serenity 静). The ultimate purpose of tai chi is to cultivate the qi or life energy within us to flow smoothly and powerfully throughout the body. The essential principles include mind integrated with the body; control of movements and breathing; generating internal energy, mindfulness, song (loosening 松) and jing (serenity 静). The ultimate purpose of tai chi is cultivate the qi or life energy within us to flow smoothly and powerfully throughout the body

Telepathy:

Telepathy is defined as communication between minds. When you can read your twin sister's thoughts without her saying a word, this is an example of telepathy. From the Greek τῆλε, tele meaning "distant" and πάθος, pathos or - patheia meaning "feeling, perception, passion, affliction, experience") is the purported vicarious transmission of information from one person to another without using any known human sensory channels or physical interaction.

Theories:

When you have a theory, you have a set of beliefs or principles that might not be proven yet. ... A theory is a set of accepted beliefs or organized principles that explain and guide analysis and one of the ways that theory is defined is that it is different from practice, when certain principles are tested.

Transcendent:

The definition of transcendent is extraordinary or beyond human experience. Talking to God is an example of a transcendent experience. Exceeding usual limits: surpassing. Extending or lying beyond the limits of ordinary experience.

Transforming:

Transformation is a fundamental change in a person's sacred or spiritual life. ... Paloutzian says that "spiritual transformation constitutes a change in the meaning system that a person holds as a basis for self-definition, the interpretation of life, and overarching purposes and ultimate concerns."

True Self:

The true self is the actual consciousness and awareness of one's self. That's what a being actually think or know they are. This contrasts with other self consciousness:
other self and ideal self. ... In the nutshell, true-self is who you know yourself to be other than who you wish you were.

U

Unconditional Love:
To define unconditional love is to say that a person loves someone unselfishly, that he or she cares about the happiness of the other person and will do anything to help that person feel happiness without expecting anything in return. In other words, the definition of unconditional love is "love without conditions."

Unconventional:
If you describe a person or their attitude or behavior as unconventional, you mean that they do not behave in the same way as most other people in their society. They are seen as being unconventional geniuses. He was known for his unconventional behavior.

Universe:
The Universe is everything we can touch, feel, sense, measure or detect. It includes living things, planets, stars, galaxies, dust clouds, light, and even time. ... The Universe contains billions of galaxies, each containing millions or billions of stars. The space between the stars and galaxies is also considered part of the universe.

V

Vibrations:
Vibration means quickly moving back and forth (or up and down) about a point of equilibrium. The vibration may be periodic (having a pattern) or random. Something that is vibrating may shake at the same time. ... This vibration will send sound waves to the ear and to the brain. "Your 'vibration' is a fancy way of describing your overall state of being. Everything in the universe is made up of energy vibrating at different frequencies. Even things that look solid are made up of vibrational energy fields at the quantum level.Vision:
Your personal vision is how you commit to living your life. It influences all areas including family, spirituality, physical well-being, leisure, and work.

Vulnerability:

Vulnerability is the quality of being easily hurt or attacked. Some seniors think it's funny to pick on the ninth graders because of their vulnerability. Vulnerability comes from the Latin word for "wound," vulnus. Vulnerability is the state of being open to injury, or appearing as if you are.

W

Wisdom:

There is a story in the Bible that speaks of Solomon, a young man who, after God offered him anything his heart desired, he requested wisdom. ... The Webster's Unabridged Dictionary defines wisdom as "knowledge, and the capacity to make due use of it."

Woo Woo:

A person readily accepting supernatural, paranormal, occult, or pseudoscientific phenomena, or emotion-based beliefs and explanations. That reporter is a bit of a woo woo. (slang) Those beliefs. He is really into all that woo woo.

Y

Yoga:

The literal meaning of the Sanskrit word Yoga is 'Yoke'. Yoga can therefore be defined as a means of uniting the individual spirit with the universal spirit of God. According to Maharishi Patanjali, Yoga is the suppression of modifications of the mind.

Spiritual Healing:

Spiritual healing can be defined more than one way.